NAVIGATING ENTREPRENEURSHIP

Secrets to Put You On
An Unstoppable Course

compiled by
Cathy Alessandra

Alessandra Media Group LLC
Los Angeles, CA
www.AlessandraMediaGroup.com

ISBN: 1497376459
ISBN-13: 978-1497376458
Library of Congress Control Number: 2014905367
CreateSpace Independent Publishing Platform
North Charleston, South Carolina

Disclaimer: At the time of printing, all email and website addresses were valid. Due to the fast-paced nature of the internet and navigating entrepreneurship, some of these may change or cease to exist.

DEDICATION

This book is dedicated to all the women who have a passion, a desire, and a calling to create the business of their dreams and live a life they love. The time is now. There are no more excuses. It's your turn in the driver's seat!

ACKNOWLEDGMENT

This book includes the stories of amazing women entrepreneurs. These are women who had a dream, a vision, and a purpose – and did it no matter what! They got behind the wheel in the driver's seat and took the road sometimes less traveled.

There is no straight path – the road is bumpy and filled with twists, turns and potholes. Sometimes you slow down for the curves, and other times you step on the gas and accelerate full speed. Here these women share their challenges and successes – with tips and ideas for you to navigate the road of entrepreneurship!

This book was the concept of innovative woman Cathy Alessandra, an entrepreneur on a mission to bring the real life stories of everyday women creating a successful business on their terms.

INTRODUCTION

Welcome to the journey of Entrepreneurship. While you may think there is a final destination – measured by the number of clients, amount of sales or balance in your bank account– the fact is that it is a continuous journey.

Being a successful entrepreneur means you think ahead of the curve and outside the box. You are continuously evaluating what is working – and what is not. You are shifting, tweaking and adjusting as you move along. There is no straight road from point A to B. It is a road filled with twists and turns, potholes and dead ends, overheated engines and ice covered bridges. And once you get to point B, you may realize you have to go back for something you forgot…. Or it's time to move on to the next pit stop.

Even the wealthiest entrepreneurs are not sitting back in their big chairs saying "well, that's done". No – they are looking for what is next, how they can improve their product or service and serve their customers even better.

When I began my first company over 18 years ago, we did not have a website. And neither did 95% of businesses. Email was not used like it is today and there were no email marketing strategies. The world of business and technology is moving fast – and you have to stay ahead, or at least keep up.

Entrepreneurship is not for the faint of heart. It takes hard work, dedication and a love for what you are doing! The stories you'll find in this book show the dedication, drive and love of these authors/entrepreneurs. They are on the road, the journey, of being an entrepreneur. They are not done. They haven't "arrived" at their final destination. They continue on their course – making stops and adjustments as necessary. And that is what puts them on an unstoppable course.

Join me as we navigate together.

TABLE OF CONTENTS

Quit? That Never Occurred to Me! 91
By Michele Pariza Wacek

IT'S NOT A STRAIGHT ROAD BUT RATHER A WILD RIDE

By Cathy Alessandra

I have always had the entrepreneurial spirit. From lemonade stands as a child to selling cosmetics as a young woman, I knew I wanted to be my own boss, have control of my destiny and create something that was all mine. And in 1995, I stumbled into my first business.

I worked in the corporate world for 8 years before having my first child. I was married at 22 and we moved a few times for my husband's career in those early years. I sold cosmetics, I sold floral arrangements at craft fairs, and I sold toys at home parties. But it wasn't until I had 2 of my 3 children that I stumbled across a need – and created a six figure business!

I launched my first company, What's Up For Kids, in 1995 with a 3 year old, a 1 year old and one soon to be on the way. The focus of my company was a print newsletter serving families in my local community. As a mom of young children, I created what I knew was needed around a topic I was passionate about – having fun with my kids.

The company grew and I was able to work when I wanted, around the schedule of my kids, from my home office. There were lots of late nights when the kids were young, but I loved owning and running a business. Everything from making the sales calls to going to the bank, I thrived on being an entrepreneur.

1

But in the summer of 2008, I hit a low! My kids were growing up and moving into high school. I had served my time at the elementary school being PTA President, Fundraiser Chair—and all the other things mothers do! I wanted more but I didn't know what that was.

While away on vacation for a few days with my family, I read the book "Distinctively Diva: Every Woman's Guide to Outrageous Living" written by four ladies; Elena Bates, Maureen O'Crean, Molly Thompson and Carilyn Vaile. The book is set up in 52 chapters. The idea is to read one chapter a week and make transformations over a year. Examples of chapters include Week 4: Acknowledge the Goddess Within; Week 7: Passion; Week 8: Freedom; Week 16: From Regret to Opportunity. And Week 52: Celebration! You get the idea—52 weeks of stories, inspirations and action plans.

Well, I read the book in the 4 days I was away. Who could wait an entire year? I was totally reenergized. I came back a new woman—re-motivated and feeling amazing about myself and my life and ready to create something new. Unknowingly, I had opened my heart and mind to the Universe and I began a journey of self-discovery!

During that time, I learned about the book *Think and Grow Rich* by Napoleon Hill and *The Success Principles* by Jack Canfield. I learned about mentors and masterminds groups. I started listening to audios about finding your passion, growing your business and opening your heart and mind to the possibilities before you. By listening to mentors and coaches and sharing it with my mastermind partners, I was able discover a new passion to connect and serve entrepreneur moms! I had been an entrepreneur mom for over 14 years. I had a very successful business. I knew what type of support I had needed and couldn't find. So in February of 2009, the National Association of Entrepreneur Moms was born—to empower moms to pursue their passion and create a balanced life.

But two years into the association, I felt that same low coming back. I was working many hours with little results. My frustration about the business was beginning to far outweigh my passion. I was attracting and trying to serve mompreneurs who were "hobbyists". Most were dabbling in something rather than committed to a hugely successful business. I had considered myself a mompreneur – after all, I had raised 3 children while raising a business.

One afternoon in a conversation with my coach, I was yet again sharing my frustration with her. Joy asked me one question that changed the course of everything. "Have you ever thought of publishing a magazine for women entrepreneurs instead?" Why was I trying to recreate the wheel? I can publish a magazine in my sleep (well, almost!). I had been doing so for 15 years! And the women's magazine was born!

It began as Today's Entrepreneur Woman – with articles, tips and tools for women entrepreneurs. It didn't take long however for another media giant with a similar name to send me a cease and desist letter. So, I changed the name to Today's Womanpreneur. Nope – that was too close as well per that media giant's team of lawyers. Then the questioning began. Was I doing the right thing? Was the Universe sending me a message saying "give it up Cathy!" Was I supposed to move forward?

I decided the answer was YES – and that it was just the journey to get there. You see, the road is NEVER straight. There are always twists and turns, steep uphill battles and fast moving downgrades that seem like they may never end. But the journey is part of the success. Because I realized if I had not had the association, I would not have met many of the amazing women entrepreneurs I had. And some of them went on to be my experts, my mastermind partners, my collaborative partners and more. I had to travel the road to success.

Since then, I have become involved in a few mastermind programs that truly changed the course of my life and business – and have taken me to a whole new level! I truly believe the opportunity to become involved in these masterminds were presented because I was open and ready to move forward, say YES and create great things.

Was the journey worth it? YES! I have created a successful business, on my terms. Doing what I love while surrounded and supported by those I love. I have created a lifestyle that fits me and my family.

So, how did I get to that point? I had my ups and downs, my successes and failures, but when evaluating how I have created all of this, there are a few key ingredients I'd like to share with you.

FOLLOW YOUR PASSION

First, I followed my passion. With both companies, I began them based on an idea that I felt passionate about. Funny enough, they both serve women. You need to love what you are doing, be on fire, ready to jump out of bed and create. By creating a business around your passion, you are creating a life, not a J-O-B. You may need to tweak things a bit to have your passion generate the income you desire, but if you aren't excited about heading to your desk, you will burn out quickly. Find your passion and live it!

BALANCE AND BOUNDARIES

The next ingredient is balance. And as I have said many times before, balance does not have to mean 50/50. As an entrepreneur, a 50/50 balance is almost impossible to achieve. You are setting yourself up for "super woman fatigue". Life is often overwhelming with your roles as mom, caretaker, philanthropist, partner, friend, taxi driver, cook, maid, volunteer and CEO, CFO, marketing director, web designer, blogger and more all screaming for your attention. Balance to me is when I feel in harmony with all parts of my life focusing on different things when needed. For example, when I began my first business, if I was able to give 30% to my business and 70% to my family and personal time, I was happy. I was in balance. My family also knows that during certain times of the year, my business requires 75% or more of my time and attention, and as long as that doesn't last too long,

I am in balance as well. Determine what your balance percentages are – where are you comfortable, maybe they shift during different times of the year or even month, but know what makes you happy and strive for that.

One tool to help you remain in balance is setting boundaries- boundaries with friends, family and even your partner. As a home-based business, I learned that hard way. When I began my business, I didn't act as if I owned a company, that I was the CEO. I was available when anyone called, any-time – to volunteer, have lunch with a friend, etc. I quickly learned that to be taken seriously as a business owner and have the time to devote to the growth of my business as well as my personal and family time, I needed to set the same boundaries as a mom who worked outside the home – office hours and days available, not answering the home phone whenever it rang and participating in the things I wanted to, that were important to me and making exceptions when I could. This included explaining to my children and family that when I am in my office with the door closed, to be respect-ful upon entering knowing I am most likely working or on the phone. But my schedule was also set up so that usually I was done working when the kids came home from school and I respected that boundary by not answer-ing the business line when I could hear it ringing in my office!

LEVERAGE ISN'T JUST FOR BUSINESS

This leads me to the next ingredient which is to leverage your life. Leverage isn't just for business anymore! As entrepreneurs, we try to do it all, see it all, be it all and then fail miserably. We need a team behind us, to support us – and then to the outside world it looks like we have it all together. I would say with almost 100% certainty that most of the other successful women who have written for this book have navigated through leveraging their life in some way. They may have a personal assistant to help with er-rands like picking up the dry cleaning, or they may order groceries online. I have hired someone to clean my house each week – a couple extra sales calls and I have more then paid for her help! And there is no reason the family can't get involved. As my kids grew older, they would start dinner and when they got their drivers license they would even do some of the grocery shopping (any excuse to take the car!).

There are ways to automate your life by ordering gifts and clothing online and setting up reminders in your online calendar. There are companies where you can put in birthdays and special occasions and they will automatically send out a personal card and gift! No missed birthdays! Having a family online calendar that everyone can access has been an essential tool for our family. My business meetings and personal appointments are on the calendar, the days off of school, the kids' appointments and classes, my husband's appointments – all in one place online that everyone can access so that other things can be scheduled without conflicts.

HONOR YOURSELF

The final ingredient is to honor you and your needs. It has been proven and you know in your heart that there is a connection between the state of your mind and the health of your body. Many things play into this – your mood, your stress level, the people you surround yourself with and others. We all have stress and overwhelm. In this high-stress society in which we live, it can be hard to step away from the stress. But its effects can take a toll on our body and mind. Scheduling time to take care of you and reduce your stress is essential. And yes, it needs to be scheduled. A daily stress reducer could include journaling, meditating, listening to music and exercising, or doing yoga. A bigger release could be a trip to the spa or a girl's weekend or couples weekend away. It is important in this environment of "chronic stress" that we schedule the time to do the things to help relieve it, make us happy and brings us joy. That also includes surrounding yourself with friends who understand and support you, not the negative energy drains. You know who they are – the ones who never have anything positive to say, are always complaining and never stop to truly support you in your life's work. Surround yourself with positive, supportive people who will help you in honoring YOU!

Being an entrepreneur has had its fill of challenges, but I am also filling my desire to create something special and even leave a legacy. My kids have gone from tots to teens and almost adult. They have seen me struggle, they have supported me by even working in the business at times. I can only hope that I have instilled in them the importance of doing something you love and peaked their interest in being an entrepreneur.

ABOUT THE AUTHOR:

Cathy Alessandra is a dynamic speaker, best-selling author, radio host and the Chief Innovative Officer of Alessandra Media Group LLC. Since 1995, she has published the successful niche magazine, *What's Up For Kids™* serving families in Los Angeles. In 2011, she took her expertise in publishing, marketing and business to launch *Today's Innovative Woman™*, creating a niche magazine serving smart, savvy women business owners. Additionally, Cathy hosts the weekly podcast radio show, Innovative Women in Business, interviewing successful women entrepreneurs and she also published the #1 Amazon bestseller, *Millionaire Moms in the Making*. Cathy was awarded the 2014 Anita Roddick Entrepreneur Award – Women Making History by the Business Women's Mega Mixer, the 2013 Spirit Award from Worthwhile Referral Services, 2012 Leading Moms in Business award by StartUp Nation, the 2011 Top 50 Mompreneur's of the Year award by Babble.com, was a finalist for the 2011 Ali Brown Platinum Excellence Award, and received the President's Call to Service Life-Time Achievement award. She has been featured on CBS.com, career-intelligence.com and KFWB news radio in Los Angeles. She speaks on stages around the country on topics ranging from marketing to her YES I CAN inspirational movement. You can read more about Cathy at www.CathyAlessandra.com.

Cathy Alessandra
Alessandra Media Group, LLC
Publisher of Today's Innovative Woman and
What's Up For Kids magazines

(888) 544-1042
www.TodaysInnovativeWoman.com
www.WhatsUpForKids.com
cathy@alessandramediagroup.com

THE DIRECTION OF YOUR DREAMS

By Chris Atley

> "Go Confidently in the Direction of Your Dreams.
> Live the Life You've Imagined."
> - Thoreau

I loved this quote the minute I saw it. I was taking big leaps in my professional life, and when I came across it I knew it was another sign from the universe that I was on the right path. Following a dream to move to a new country *and* creating a business I was passionate about.

Running a business is hard. We're forced to deal with our own stuff. We must go against the status quo, have faith in our dreams when others don't, and let go of what other people think of us. This is a challenge to say the least. I like to say that running a business is the *best* personal development course a person can take.

I struggled for the first five years I was in business. It wasn't until year 6 (in 2013), that I broke through and started creating the income I *knew* I was capable of. It was quite a journey. It was heart wrenching, shame inducing and a road filled with more up's and down's then I care to remember. BUT I can say this; it's been worth every single second. It's brought me to where I am today. Sharing my gifts on a bigger scale, and connecting with heart-centered business owners like you.

I know what it's like to worry and I also know what it takes to break through. I've learned that when we have the courage to step-up, the universe is right there with us. Showing us the way to make our dreams come true. Always and without fail. I believe this is possible for you too. It's up to you to decide though - are you willing to go for it? To play bigger than you ever thought possible? Let's find out.

I am going to share my story with you on how I found my passion, learned to dream big and stopped settling for less. The lessons I've learned are integral to building a six-figure business and becoming a happier person. My hope is that you see what is possible for you, and have the courage and inspiration to go for it!

PASSION SEEKING

After earning a bachelor's degree in psychology at Wilfred Laurier University in Canada, I started working in the insurance industry. I took lots of courses, moved-up quickly and was making good money. Within a few years, I was negotiating large liability and property claims, and even working on the coveted Province of Ontario account. I learned a lot, but something was missing. I was seeing people at their worst and it was adversarial to say the least.

I started a new search. I would watch movies about human rights and the justice system, and get really worked up! I had a fire inside of me that wanted to break down old systems, and make the world a better place. I realized I didn't have this enthusiasm for my current career. I had this longing to feel passionate about my job, my life - to take a stand for something. I didn't want to settle. The problem was that I couldn't seem to find what that was.

THE AWAKENING

I ended up getting pregnant while we were on vacation in Greece, which was a welcomed surprise after getting over the initial shock! Our little guy decided to make his appearance 3-weeks early, which happened to be on moving day. I literally had the movers wait to move our bedroom last so that I had somewhere to have contractions! After lots of unpacking, sleepless nights and navigating through various renovations, we were finally starting to feel settled in our new home with our new baby boy.

I can still remember the day clearly. I was waiting for a couple of girlfriend's to arrive, when all of a sudden my Mom showed-up. She lived a street over, but didn't usually just pop-by unannounced. So that was strange. Before she could explain what she was doing there, my husband came home from work. Even stranger. He asked me to come into our bedroom and that's when he told me my Dad had died. My Dad had been living in Cambodia at the time, where he was spending his retirement from his teaching career. He died from liver sclerosis at age 57. This was a shock and a surprise. He was an alcoholic and we had tried intervening. It didn't work, and he ended up putting a lot of distance between himself and his family. I had no idea just how bad things were. It was a terrible, terrible feeling. Knowing I would never see him again and that was it. For more on this story and what I went on to learn about life after death, you can download my audio course for free at: www.chrisatley/freecourse

From there it was a whirlwind. My parents had been divorced for a long time, and even though I had a lot of support from my Mom and Dad's side of the family, I felt very alone in the handling of his affairs. For awhile we couldn't even find the paperwork outlining what would happen when he passed. It was a very stressful time while navigating this process and with taking care of a newborn. Breast-feeding went out the window pretty fast.

The next few months were rough. I was pretty angry. Angry that my Dad would let himself get to the point of death, that the intervention I conducted failed and that my Dad never met our son Jude. Just plain angry about life in general to be honest.

DREAM BIG!

Many months later, while still being off on maternity leave, I ended up going to lunch with a girlfriend. I can still remember the place we went to and the sandwich I ate. We had such a great time and I felt rejuvenated afterward! So much so, that when I got home I decided to watch the movie "The Secret". My Mom had given it to me a month prior and I just couldn't seem to make myself watch it. Looking back it's no coincidence that it took being in a good mood to watch the movie, since positive attracts positive. For more on this spiritual law and others, download a free audio course at: www.chrisatley/freecourse

I watched the movie that day and it forever changed my life! I was blown away. I had no idea we could create whatever we wanted. Looking back over my life it made sense, but I didn't understand just how much control we actually had over it. After this everything changed. In the movie they say to **follow your bliss** - for me this was palm trees, sunshine and the ocean. I knew deep in my heart that I wanted to move to California. I started asking different questions, like why couldn't I move? Why did I have to stay where I grew-up? Why couldn't I create where I wanted to live first, and not the other way around like most people do and move because of a job? I was lucky my husband was excited and on-board with this plan.

The movie started my love affair with the law of attraction and personal growth. After watching the movie, I read everything I could get my hands on. I was fascinated and I quickly realized my life purpose – to understand this, master it and help others do the same. This I was immensely passionate about. This is what I would take a stand for.

MAKE THE DECISION

Doors kept opening for me because I made a *decision* to do something different. The decision to do something is one of the **most important steps**. You do not need the opportunity to show-up unless you decide to do it. A lot of people stay stuck in the decision making process, which can be debilitating. Think about what you really want and go for it even though it's a little scary! The universe will always support you and show you your next steps.

I ended up learning about coaching and knew it was the perfect fit! After hiring a coach and making unexpected changes in my own life - like going for regular massages, date nights and walks in nature - I decided to take a coaching certification course in Chicago. I still practice these acts of self-care to this day and it's just as important to my success as breathing. Really.

BE FLEXIBLE

Opportunities were flying left, right and center to learn how to set-up a business. I ended up becoming a leader in this area. I always thought I would help people make career changes since this is what I did, BUT the **universe had other plans** for me. I was naturally attracting other business owners who were a few steps behind me, and wanted to learn what I was doing. The way things have unfolded for me have been **divinely guided** and I love what I am doing now with business owners. It truly makes my heart sing.

After months of working at my insurance job, and juggling coaching clients along with the demands of being a parent, I decided to quit and run my business full-time. I was there for 10 years to the day. It was one of the biggest decisions I've ever had to make and I was literally sick to my stomach over it. Looking back, I cannot imagine NOT making that decision.

With my coaching business up and running, I was still working hard at making my dream of living in California come true. I was practicing what I was learning about the law of attraction on a daily basis. An amazing job opportunity presented itself for my husband, but much to my dismay, we weren't ready to go - yet.

FOLLOWING YOUR DREAMS ISN'T ALWAYS EASY

It takes a lot of courage and strength to stay with our dreams. Especially when the road doesn't always seem easy. Isn't everything **supposed to flow** with the law of attraction if you're on the right path? Wrong and double wrong. What's missing in "the Secret" is the personal development piece. The opportunity is always there for us to have what we want, but if we're overcome with fear and limiting beliefs, we will not see it. We have to re-move our own inner obstacles in order to see the magic. I had to let go of the guilt of leaving family and realize it was okay to follow my dreams. I had to learn how to set boundaries and take care of myself. I also learned when we make time for ourselves it keeps our vibration high, so that we can see all of the wonderful opportunities waiting for us. For more on how to fully harness this type of energy, download my audio course at: www. chrisatley/freecourse

ENDLESS POSSIBILITIES

The same job opportunity my husband had turned down a year prior came up again. Funny how that works. I love the way Marianne Williamson explains this in her book, "The Divine Law of Compensation". She says the universe is like a GPS. When we get off course it will redirect us back to where we want to go. The universe often has a **way bigger plan for us** than we could ever dream up ourselves.

GET OUT OF YOUR OWN WAY

After taking some time to get our family set-up post move, I was ready to hit the ground running with my business. I had all of the tools, so I thought it would be a piece of cake. It was to some extent in that I was teaching workshops at some of the top universities in the country and building my entrepreneurial community. Things were happening. So why wasn't my income soaring the way it should be?

Other business owners were asking me how I was doing it. Boy, did I have them fooled. It "looked" like I was a successful businesswoman. I was successful in that I was getting out there and making things happen. What wasn't happening was a rise in my bank account. Money would come, but it would also go. It wasn't consistent, and when it would start coming in, it would stop almost as fast. I was barely making $11000.00 a year! There is no way I could admit this though! The shame I felt around this and the lack of confidence was **unbearable** at times. Especially in a world where our worth is measured by our bank accounts and accomplishments.

When things were great and money was flowing, I felt awesome! On the flip side, when it wasn't, I felt like a failure. I would learn later I was **measuring my self-worth by my bank account**. I share this with you now because it has to stop. We are all beautiful people with amazing gifts that need to be shared with the world. Our bank accounts are not how we should be measuring our worth. However, I will say that our bank accounts show us exactly where we need to grow. That is if we're not where we want to be financially.

I came to realize if I wasn't getting the results I wanted in my business, **I was the problem**. Even though I logically understood and believed in the law of attraction – and had some pretty great results like moving to a new country - something was off when it came to my business. By this time, my inheritance money was all gone. Looking back – it's funny because I would always convince myself that if I took just one more program I would be **fixed** and that would be the last investment. I've come to realize that I will always be learning and growing, and the support will be ongoing. The minute I stop learning, is the second I start dying.

So I decided to invest in a really big coaching program with a coach who specialized in universal law. I'm talking a BIG investment. I could have purchased a really nice car. I had no idea how I was going to pull it off, but I knew I *had* to do it. This was the start of me truly breaking free. I was able to discover my biggest fear and what was *really* holding me back from having the business and life I wanted. I talk a lot more about this in my audio course, "Learn How to Turn Your Annual Income to Your Monthly Income in 30-minutes a Day", which you can download for free at: www.chrisatley/freecourse

SURRENDER & HAVE FAITH, YOUR SUCCESS IS CERTAIN

Within a month and half of doing this deeper work, I was able to triple my income, in month 8 I generated more income then I had earned in the entire year before, and within 10 months I had generated a 6-figure business!! This year I'm already on track to earning multiple 6-figures in just the first quarter!

To be honest though, the money part of it is fun and enables me to do great things, but that's not what it's really about. It just symbolizes the internal changes that took place in order to achieve those outside results. What changed is that I started *believing in myself*. I wasn't seeing my own worth. Once I was able to get out of my own way I could see all of the opportunities right there that the law of attraction promises. If you don't believe in yourself, you will not see what is available for you. Some opportunities had literally been sitting right in front of me for months! To get help shifting your own roadblocks, visit: www.chrisatley/freecourse to download your free audio course filled with great exercises.

I also had to learn how to let go of controlling *how* the opportunity would happen, and trust that it would. This is the **same lesson** I learned with moving. It continues to be one of my biggest lessons, and I am challenged with it at every big step I take. Thankfully the more I create the easier it gets.

I share my results with you because I want you to know it *is* possible for you too. The universe doesn't decide that I get 1 million and you get $5.00. It doesn't work like that. It is available for everyone. If you have the business basics down, and still aren't getting the results you want, the problem is inside not outside.

I was working with a client recently who was earning more than 6-figures already, but still wasn't where she wanted to be. We started doing some digging. We looked at the beliefs that were holding her back and dug deep into the past to find out where they were coming from. In an hour we were able to determine that it was a self-worth issue. She had been abused as a child, and there was a lot of pain around this. She had a major breakthrough in just one session. After only 2-months of working together, she generated $120,000.00 in new business! Going deep works, and it works quickly. BUT you have to be open and willing to go there. You also have to be willing to change your environment and behaviors to support your new beliefs. This is a process. Not many people are willing to go there. They will use any excuse in the book to not do what it takes. The number one excuse is money. If we truly believe in abundance then why are we saying no because of the money? This is where we need to **breakthrough**.

HAPPINESS

As a result of doing this deeper work, I've made A LOT of changes in my personal life. The biggest is that I've stopped worrying about money. I've been able to hire someone consistently to help with house cleaning and laundry, an accountant to help me manage both business and personal finances, and a business manager to help me implement systems and have the support I need to help even more people! These hires are special because not only have my husband and I both got our time back, I am giving other people jobs. I am having a ripple effect and this is worth every single struggle there was!

I now know I have the power to create. I know I am always taken care of. After so many positive experiences, it's hard not to and you can have them too. This change in thinking has led to more loving relationships with my kids and my husband. I feel free. I now have the beliefs and self-worth that match my bigger vision. I work with the most amazing heart-centered business owners, and I'm helping them break-free too! This is what I take a stand for. That we don't have to settle for less, and that anything and everything is possible. Just say yes!

ABOUT THE AUTHOR:

Chris Atley shows entrepreneurs how to make better decisions so they can get different results. Chris inspires thousands of entrepreneurs internationally through her writing, teaching and coaching programs. Her mission is to help as many people as she can create fabulous businesses and freedom-filled lives! Chris is a certified coach, NLP-Practitioner and has a BA in Psychology. She walks the talk, and draws on her own experience to help others build successful businesses.

Chris has a unique ability to identify the obstacles that keep business owners stuck - that they often aren't even aware of! She helps people go deep to shift their blocks, and then shows them how to use their own resources to make different decisions and create lasting change. Chris is a wiz at helping business owners get results fast - often during their first call! Connect with Chris and receive special gifts at: www.chrisatley.com.

Chris Atley

(858) 367-9217
www.chrisatley.com
support@chrisatley.com

YES THERE IS A GPS TO SUCCESS!

By Bibi Goldstein

"What did I get myself into?" I cannot begin to tell you how many times I have asked myself that question over the past 8 years. The answer is always the same... "Freedom, my kind of freedom", financial, time, creative, whatever happens to be important to me at that moment, and believe me that will be different at various junctures of this adventure. You will second guess yourself as often as you allow. I didn't trust my gut when I should have, and have some regrets because of that.

FEAR AND PASSION

When I started my business, I did so with a business partner because I was afraid to do it on my own. This turned out to be a learning experience on which I didn't really need to be educated. I had loved ones who believed in me more than I believed in myself, who told me to do it on my own, but I was so crippled with the thought of flying the plane solo that I put myself in a situation I would never wish upon anyone. Trust your gut and fight your fear, live in the moment and you'll feel the adrenaline when you make a decision that feels scary, but you are compelled to do it anyway.

I love what my business represents for other small businesses, but most importantly, I love that it allows me to have that very similar feeling of contributing which volunteerism gives me. Having the opportunity to support small business owners when they feel totally overwhelmed and don't know where to start with a project or a task is so gratifying for me. I finally understood when my business coach asked, "If you weren't paid a penny for what you do, would you still do it?" YES! YES! Absolutely YES!

Don't get me wrong, there are plenty of days that I feel like throwing in the towel or want to crawl back in bed and not deal with another challenge that faces the business or me. Passion, real passion for what you do means that you allow yourself to get lost every once in a while. Find out what gets you back on track, consciously have a plan to identify when you seem to detour, then put that plan into action. When I have these moments, it mostly stems from the feeling of overwhelm coming on, or clutter, either physical or mental. Given that I'm in the business of helping people out of overwhelm, I developed a quick and easy way to help several of my clients, and myself, out of it. My "15 Minutes From Overwhelmed To Organized" system helps me every time; it allows me to deconstruct what feels like a mess and to create the opportunity to systematically remove the things that are creating overwhelm and/or clutter for me. Use it now and as often as you need to help yourself get back to that place of passion, seeing the big picture rather than get stuck in the tasks and the day to day.

BOARD OF ADVISORS

On almost any road trip you're going to come across some bridges. I don't like bridges. Ask anyone who knows me; I absolutely don't like driving over them. I do however love the bridges that have been part of my journey as an entrepreneur. There will be countless times that you will find yourself stuck, trying to figure out how to get on the other side of the current day's challenge. If there is nothing else you take from the story of my journey, please remember this – you must have your own board of advisors giving you unbiased, honest (sometimes brutally honest) and creative advice. I read the book "Think and Grow Rich" by Napoleon Hill in the first few years I was in business, and have read it several times since, because it reminds me often that the fundamentals of business are the same as they were in 1937 when that book was written. More importantly, it never lets me forget that what I think, even if I don't verbalize those thoughts, has a direct relationship to the outcome. There are two specific ways I keep a board of advisors: I participate in two different mastermind groups (one paid, one free) of women who are in various stages of their business, and I have a business coach.

There are many schools of thought when it comes to masterminds, some feel that if you don't pay for it, there is not enough commitment to the group, others feel that everyone in the group should be at a higher level than you so that you are benefiting from their experiences. I do not necessarily believe in either of those philosophies. I have learned so much from the business owners in my free mastermind group who are just starting out in their businesses, because they are my ideal client and it is their perspective I want. My paid mastermind gives me incredible insight on business trends, technology, marketing and financial aspects of my business. Both give me guidance from the heart, with honesty, which is most important to me. Choose whatever works for you, but get involved with a mastermind group that allows for you to have enough time to work through specific challenges or projects each time you meet. An added benefit is that we all feel good about ourselves when we contribute, and I like that feeling of being a part of the growth of someone else's business.

I have had the same business coach for over 5 years, Joy Chudacoff of Smart Women Smart Solutions. Again, there are multiple opinions about this, and believe me I have heard them all. Here is my gauge of whether I need to look for another coach, when I have had no growth or movement in a positive direction for either myself or my business AFTER I have done everything she guided me to, then it is time to move on. I have watched Joy's business evolve and grow over the years I have worked with her, and that is important to me also, that shows me that she practices what she preaches. I use my time with Joy as purposefully as possible; there are times when she is my therapist (those are few but necessary). Most uses of our time together are working through a program I'm developing, revamping my organizational structure or evaluating my service offerings and reviewing my financials. I encourage you to have a plan with your coach, I have seen many friends and clients spend literally thousands of dollars and not fully take advantage of what they are paying for. Do your due diligence when you are deciding to work with a coach. Talk to others who have coached with them, the happy ones and the not so happy ones. You can find them on your own, or your potential coach may be willing to share this information. You would contact references for someone taking care of your children, why wouldn't you do the same for your future and that of your business?

COMMUNITY AND REPUTATION

One of the biggest lessons I learned early on was about how important community was to my business. Local and online communities are crucial to creating a reputation, brand and fans for your business. I got involved with my local chamber of commerce and joined women-centric committees that allowed me to focus on causes that were important to me, but gave me opportunities to showcase my business and network at the same time. Be careful not to let anything become too consuming of your time, it is important to keep balance in mind. Remember that when you are willing to give your time, there is always someone willing to take it.

Online communities can be a bit more complicated, mostly in how they come about. There are several platforms and opportunities to sit behind the computer and interact with people on social media. Remember that you can still affect your reputation depending how, and with whom you interact. Be very aware of the associations you make for yourself in these communities; believe me, other people are. I learned this lesson when there was a business associate I was connected with who would continuously post and interact on social media by complaining and describing situations that showed their clients in a negative light. I had referred a client to this associate and the client did some research, checking them out on Facebook etc. What she found with these negative comments made her question me and how I could make a referral to someone who clearly did not understand why this was not professional. Putting your thoughts in writing without a filter could come back to bite you, putting that writing on the internet will definitely come back to bite you.

GOALS AND PLANS

I am someone who always needs to know where my destination is and how far I am from it. Knowing where the turns and the traffic are, somehow it makes me feel better when I know what is coming up. So having a plan, a map that gives you a clear path to your goals, is crucial to every business. Having realistic and attainable goals that you set incrementally throughout the year, as well as long-term (three and five years) goals, will help to keep you on track. Focus on the plan to reach those goals, work your way backwards to see what you need to implement, delegate, remove, reduce, increase or change.

Without goals and a plan to reach them, your business will be like a race car on a track going in circles, the only objective being to finish the most laps the quickest. In theory that sounds like you have won the race, but business sustainability has nothing to do with finishing first, and everything to do with staying on the track the longest.

ABOUT THE AUTHOR:

Bibi Goldstein is the owner of Buying Time, LLC, a personal and virtual assistant service providing business owners and individuals support for their administrative needs, event coordination and time management and delegation strategies. An active member of her business community in the South Bay of Los Angeles. Bibi is current President of the South Bay Business Women's Association, she served as a committee member (2008-2012) and past chair (2011-2012) for the Manhattan Beach Women In Business, past President of the Kiwanis Club of Manhattan Beach, and a member of the 2011 class of Leadership Redondo Beach. Bibi has co-authored Get Organized Today and Business Success With Ease, and she continues in her third year as a contributing expert writer to Today's Innovative Woman Magazine. Bibi lives in Redondo Beach with her husband Mark while her daughter Julie is a senior at San Francisco State.

Bibi Goldstein
Buying Time LLC

(310) 376-1835
www.BuyingTimeLLC.com
bibi@buyingtimellc.com

NO "PLAN B"

By Jaime Geffner

"That's my next job!" At that moment, I knew without a shadow of a doubt that I had finally figured out what I wanted to do as a career, and exactly where I wanted to get my start. I finally felt that feeling of excitement and exhilaration, that sense of inner knowing that this was absolutely the perfect opportunity for me right now in my life. The only question was how. How would I get this job? Who did I know that could possibly help me get hired, even as an entry-level employee? How would I prove that I could contribute enough to make them want to hire me?

So what is this dream job that I'm referring to? The job that I absolutely knew in my gut was mine, even though I had no logical or rational reason to believe it to be so was: Producer for the "Dr. Phil" show.

At that time, in mid-2002, I was working as a casting director in the world of voiceover. I had a pretty good position, I was making decent money, and I enjoyed it for the most part. But I knew it wasn't what I wanted to do forever, and that I wasn't inspired enough by the day-to-day work to stay in the voiceover industry for much longer.

On the other hand, I had always been a big fan of Oprah Winfrey. I watched her daily TV talk show regularly, and of course I knew all about Dr. Phil, America's Resident Therapist, who appeared every Tuesday on "Oprah" to dish out advice in his tell-it-like-it-is style. The moment I found out that

Dr. Phil was going to be hosting his own TV talk show, and that it was going to be filmed in Los Angeles at Paramount Studios, I just knew that this was it!

So I got to work at manifesting my vision. The first thing I did was the most obvious course of action to take - I sent in my resume with a cover letter explaining why I so badly wanted to work on the show. Although I had some entertainment industry experience already, I had no real "producing" experience that would make me stand out as someone qualified to get hired on my own merit. Unfortunately, I didn't get a phone call or any type of response whatsoever to my first attempt at getting hired.

Next, I tried using every entertainment industry connection I had at the time to get me an introduction to someone on staff. Anyone and everyone who had any type of pull, or who might know someone who did, I called on for help. I tried this strategy of getting connected through a 3rd party referral for several months, with no luck.

Still determined, I decided that I needed to take my fate back into my own hands and try to make a personal connection on my own. So I attended a live event where Dr. Phil was speaking at the Universal Amphitheatre in Los Angeles. My goal was to introduce myself to the people who were there on staff, working for Dr. Phil, in hopes that one of them would be able to connect me to the right person who could hire me to work on Dr. Phil's brand new TV show. I went to the event armed with several copies of my resume, an impassioned cover letter, and most importantly, fake business cards that I had printed at home which had my job title as "Future Producer for The Dr. Phil Show." I did actually manage to meet a few producers that night who later became some of my very good friends, and one of them my first boss at "Dr. Phil", but that attempt still didn't do the trick of getting me hired.

Even though I had gotten no real or encouraging results to this point, I still desperately wanted this job - probably more than I had ever wanted anything else up to that point in my life. Despite the dismal outlook, and my seeming lack of progress at achieving my goal, I was absolutely unwilling to accept the possibility that this wasn't going to happen for me. Then I had the thought: what if I offer to work for them for free, to prove my worth and convince them that I would be an invaluable team member who they would be foolish not to hire? My last attempt was to seek out an unpaid internship on the show. I sent in my resume and thankfully I got called in for an internship interview. This was my big chance. I was way overqualified to be an intern. I was also a few years older than most other applicants, since I had already graduated college 3 years earlier with my Bachelor's degree, and had since become a full-time member of the work force. However, I made it clear that I was willing to do whatever it took to get my foot in the door, and they were more than happy to accept my offer to provide them with free labor in exchange for the chance to make my dream a reality.

Much to my surprise, at the internship interview I was informed that even though I had already earned my college degree, I still needed to receive college credit in order to qualify for the internship. I quickly enrolled myself back into a broadcasting class at my local community college, quit my paid position as a casting director (much to the shock of my bosses, who of course thought I was making a big mistake), and got to work at the bottom of the "Dr. Phil" production staff totem pole as an unpaid intern. I didn't have a desk to sit at, a telephone to make calls from (this was before the iPhone became a household item), or even a computer of my own to work at (laptops and iPads weren't readily available back then either!) In order to complete my daily assignments, I had to get crafty. I made friends with other staff members and borrowed their workspaces while they were in meetings, out to lunch, or out of the office for the day. It was tough and in all honesty, sometimes it felt a little bit degrading, but that wasn't what I chose to focus on. I knew exactly why I was there, what I was committed to, and most importantly, that things definitely wouldn't be this way forever.

I made it my mission to introduce myself to every staff member on the show (including Dr. Phil himself), to let them know who I was, why I was there, and exactly what I wanted. It took me 3 full months of volunteering my time, working about 50 hours a week for free, until a position finally opened up that I was now qualified for. This time, I was armed with staff members who had become my co-workers, friends and allies, and were happily willing to put in a good word for me with the Executive Producer as to what an incredible asset I was and would continue to be to the team. At last, after almost being passed over for the job by another more qualified candidate, I finally got one giant step closer to my goal by getting hired as a Production Assistant on the "Dr. Phil" show!

I spent the next 5 years working my butt off. Along the way, I got promoted several times - first to Associate Producer and then to Senior Associate Producer. My job as a producer was a lot less glamorous and a lot more grueling than I had originally anticipated it would be, but I still loved every minute if it. It was truly an incredible experience that I would not trade for anything in the world.

Nevertheless, after 5 long years of countless hours at work, many sleepless nights, burning myself out in every possible way, and not seeing my husband nearly enough, I finally decided that it was time to move on. I could no longer envision myself moving up to the next level within the company, and I knew that there were other things I really wanted to accomplish. So I finished out my contract and gave my notice, even getting an open invitation to return if I ever changed my mind, and I left.

So what was next for me? As someone who has always been very invested in my own personal development, spiritual growth and self-improvement, I took some time to reflect on my experience and figure out where to go from there. I came to realize that while I thought that what I wanted was to be a producer for the "Dr. Phil" show, what I *actually* wanted was to change people's lives, to help and inspire millions of viewers, and to use my unique gifts, talents and abilities to make the world a better place to live. I absolutely loved being a producer, and the title suited my personality well. I knew for sure that I wanted to continue on that path. But I also knew that if I was going to work 24/7, I wanted it to be for myself, and on my own terms.

I didn't quite realize it then, but it turns out that my experience working for "Dr. Phil" set me up for success as an entrepreneur in many ways. It taught me to be open-minded, pushing me past my limits so often that it became normal to reach for something beyond my perceived limitations. It inspired me to have faith that no matter how unlikely something seemed to be, it always worked out exactly as it was supposed to, and for the highest good. And it gave me hope that anything is possible with a clear enough vision, a strong enough desire, and an absolute willingness to do whatever it takes, for as long as it takes, to get what you want.

I took these lessons with me into my next great venture, diving head first into the world of entrepreneurship. Becoming an entrepreneur was something I had been dreaming about for years, along with my husband and producing partner, Steve Geffner. Steve is the love of my life, my best friend and my soul mate. Ever since we first met and fell in love in 2001, we always knew that someday we wanted to find a way to work together, doing what we both love and are most passionate about. It just so happens that we have complementary training, talents and skill sets that make us an exceptionally powerful producing team! Before we met, Steve earned his Radio/TV/Film degree from Northwestern University and then moved to Hollywood to pursue his dream of working in TV production, starting his career on the Emmy Award-winning NBC sitcom, "Frasier". After getting married in 2003, we spent several hours of our honeymoon on the beach in Maui, brainstorming about our first business idea together. Although working together full time was something we aspired to from the very beginning of our relationship, it wasn't until I left "Dr. Phil" in 2007 that we formally created the vision for our production company together, and not until 2008 that we officially launched what we now call "Geffner Productions".

Similar to the challenge of getting hired at "Dr. Phil", Steve and I endured several failed attempts at success in the early days of getting our business off the ground. However, thanks in part to my "Dr. Phil" experience I knew that if I really wanted to own my own business and make it a success, I had no other choice than to keep moving forward and trust that eventually everything would work out in my favor.

Our initial vision for our company was to create and produce original TV programming that inspires people to lead extraordinary lives. We spent several years creating and pitching show ideas to networks and production companies, hoping to get our first TV show sold. Although we got extremely close on 3 separate occasions to selling 3 different show concepts to 3 different production companies, we quickly discovered that our expectations about how easy it would be to break in as show creators and producers were extremely unrealistic.

By 2010, we were broke! In a bold and unwavering attempt to pursue our dreams at all costs, we had used up our entire life savings, tapped into and cleaned out our IRA accounts, and were now faced with a big decision that would severely impact the future of our company. We could no longer afford financially to hold onto both the business we had started AND the property we had purchased back in 2007 - our very first home together, a beautiful two-bedroom condo that we had gutted, renovated and re-designed ourselves. The question was this: should we let go of the home we had built, and keep going with our dream of growing our own production company, OR hold onto our vision of being homeowners and go back to work full time for other people? After considering all possibilities, the decision became a relatively easy one for us to make – we decided to let go of the house and continue to pursue success for Geffner Productions.

At that point, we started over. Our vision for our company still remained the same, but we knew then that we had to find a different, more creative way to pursue it. Fundamentally, we had to start bringing in a steady income to keep the business alive. Thankfully, we both already had the production experience, talent and skills to do so.

In mid-2010, with a shift in perspective about what we needed to do and how we intended to accomplish it, we made a discovery that changed everything! We learned that there was a large, growing demand for creating, producing, filming and editing high-quality online video content. We realized that we could make a living by using our TV & video production skills to help entrepreneurs share their knowledge and expertise via online video, in order to expand their brand awareness, grow their businesses, and ultimately serve their life's purpose in a bigger, more impactful way. What started as a way to earn an income to keep our business alive has since turned into a huge passion of ours: helping people share their greatness with the world, via online video. As we've continued to educate ourselves about the world of online video in order to best serve our video production clients' needs, we have expanded our vision for how we can help people powerfully use online video. In early 2014, we started coaching entrepreneurs about how to create and develop a successful online video strategy that will work for their unique businesses, as well as developing online courses and a free weekly blog show to educate entrepreneurs from all over the world about how to use online video to transform their businesses.

Although we absolutely love filming videos for entrepreneurs and helping them use online video to grow their businesses, we also still have a strong desire to create our own original TV programming and share it with the world. So in late 2013, in addition to the work we continue to do with entrepreneurs through Geffner Productions (http://GeffnerProductions. com), we decided to launch Geffner TV (http://GeffnerTV.com), our own online TV channel with original programming that inspires people to greatness in their personal and professional lives. With all the experience we have acquired from nearly 4 years of producing more than 1500 videos for clients, we now have the equipment & set-up, the experience and the confidence to move forward with creating and producing our own online TV show ideas. And the best part is we don't have to wait for somebody else to give us permission to move forward with our vision. On September 3, 2013 we officially launched our online TV channel at GeffnerTV.com, with the first of many online TV show concepts designed to inspire people to create the life and lifestyle they desire, just as we have.

It has been a long road since I first decided that I wanted to be a producer and set out on my journey to become one. And without a doubt, there have been many challenges and roadblocks along the way. But there have also been many exhilarating, exciting and amazing experiences that have made me feel alive and energized, and absolutely certain that I am living my life's purpose. I know without a doubt when I am practicing the art of producing that I am doing exactly what I'm supposed to be doing in this world. The way I know for sure is there is nothing else that I can imagine myself being happy doing. Just as in my days of trying to become a producer for "Dr. Phil", I have no "Plan B", and there is no other dream planted in my heart. Simply put, there is nothing else that feels right for me to do. So I just keep going. I get up every day and I do my very best to do my great work and keep making a positive impact in the world. And through my vision of producing powerful and inspirational programming, as well as helping and inspiring others along the way, I have created success, on my own terms. I continue to make progress in the direction of my dreams every single day. And if I can do it, then I know you can too. All I started with was a clear vision, a burning desire and the unwillingness to give up. After all, the only way to truly fail at anything in life is to quit while you're still behind. As long as you're still in the game, still moving forward, still giving it your best shot, you're still on the path to success. And that is what it means to be unstoppable.

ABOUT THE AUTHOR:

Jaime Geffner is an Online Video & TV Producer, and the Co-Creator of Geffner Productions, a production company she owns and operates with her husband and producing partner, Steve Geffner. Before starting Geffner Productions, Jaime spent 5 years working as a producer for the hit daytime talk show "Dr. Phil". In 2007, she left her job at "Dr. Phil" to pursue her dream of creating and producing her own original programming ideas. In 2008, Geffner Productions was created as a way for Jaime and Steve to work together full-time, doing what they both love and are most passionate about. In 2010, Jaime and Steve began producing high-quality online video projects for private clients and large companies, helping on-camera experts and entrepreneurs share their knowledge and expertise, expand their reach, grow their businesses, and get discovered via online video. In 2013, Jaime and Steve launched Geffner TV, the home of their original episodic programming, featuring online TV shows that inspire and empower viewers to create greatness in their personal and professional lives. In 2014, Jaime and Steve expanded their vision and began educating entrepreneurs from all over the world about how to use online video to transform their businesses.

Jaime Geffner
Geffner Productions

www.GeffnerProductions.com
jaime@geffnerproductions.com

THE ENTREPRENEURIAL PATH

By Yvonne Larson

I feel I must have been born with the entrepreneurial gene. The earliest memory I have of business is when I was six years old. I went door to door selling our neighbors rocks. These were not pet rocks, these were just rocks. Can you believe that my neighbors actually bought plain old rocks from me? Well this sparked the confidence in my tiny inner business woman. I moved on to hand crafting Christmas decorations from pipe-cleaners, lace, and beads which I also sold door to door.

Then, came my most fulfilling childhood entrepreneurial memory, my fate was sealed... I had a booming lemonade business. When I say business, I don't mean a card table with a sign. One of my mom's friends crafted a full scale (for an eight year old) lemonade booth with a counter, cash drawer, roof and sign on wheels. I loved the opportunity to wheel my stand down from my house to the corner and sell my wares. I treated it like a job and it made me feel like a grown up. I was the popular hot spot the mailman and college students frequented every day.

Fast forward to my own college years, when I was approached with a home based business. In one month I had won a company challenge and got to go meet the founder and owner of that company face to face. Working with that company gave me so much core business knowledge which I've used on a daily bases ever since. Not only did I learn about the products I was selling, I learned multiple aspects of being a business owner. I learned how to set up, manage, and track my business. I learned the people skills and psychology of business. I learned that networking and marketing aren't the same thing, but go hand in hand. I found the culture and community of this company so loving and supportive. I grew as a person as I learned how to be successful in this business.

I can't imagine NOT being on an entrepreneurial path. I love so many things about being an entrepreneur. I love taking risks and throwing my hat over the fence as they say. I love the opportunities to be creative and to make things of nothing. I love creating systems, charts, grids, and promotions. I even love the element of surprise when things that did not look like they would work out somehow do. I love that it's a constant opportunity for growth. I love learning something new every day. I love choosing my destiny. I love moving from one thing to the next and being able to let things settle in around me. I love having leaders around me building teams. I love the networking, meeting new people and creating new opportunities. I love inspiring people to believe in themselves, their dreams and to release the obstacles keeping them from their joy and passion. I love searching for and finding new ways to expand myself and my business.

MY VISION OF BEING A MENTOR

In 2001, I had my first vision for being a mentor to massage therapists going into their own full time practice. In only 3 years I had acquired 600 clients and had a regular 50 hour work load with a waiting list. I knew I had something to share! I transitioned straight from my training into a successful thriving business for myself. Others I had trained with did not have such immediate success and I began reflecting on the reason. I asked myself, "why is it that I can always generate clients and create the cash I need when so many other therapists are struggling from the starving healer syndrome?" "Why have I been unstoppable in navigating entrepreneurship and how could I create a path to help?" Thus began my quest to answer and resolve this issue.

TO INCREASE INCOME YOU MUST INVEST

The first thing I realized is I am always ready to invest in myself and my business. As far back as I can remember I have craved learning, discovering, gaining new skills and acquiring every pearl of wisdom along my path. I've hired life coaches, business coaches, and requested mentors. I have purchased books, audio programs, live weekend trainings and even year-long intensives. Since some of these programs were cross country or even out of country I even had to invest in travel and hotel accommodations as well. I did whatever it took to get in front of these masters of business and transformation to squeeze out every drop of gold they were offering. I also discovered a pattern of my investments in these programs. I am willing to invest based on the degree of respect the program leader had earned as demonstrated by the size of their circle of influence. Even if it seems I already had the information they were offering, I am compelled to see how "old" information is interpreted by different people and brought to life in a new light. When I discover new leaders and trainers who are passionately on a path to empower others, I want to partner with them.

TRIED AND TRUE, WHEN OLD BECOMES NEW

Reviewing courses or signing up for training you feel you may have mastered may occur as an impractical approach, but I follow the advice of my brilliant mother concerning investing in new skills and knowledge. She said, "Always invest in yourself" and "even one new transforming pearl of wisdom is worth it".

An example of this mindset is my recent partnership with one of LA's long-standing and highly revered massage schools. In my many studies, I had the pleasure of cultivating a relationship and building trust with this incredible entrepreneurial woman. We spent 3 years in a training program in communication, team management and leadership. After a decade of developing The Massage Business Academy I met with this woman who is the owner of this prestigious school. I shared the purpose of this program and my desire to partner. Although I have taken the basic training two prior times we agreed that it would be beneficial to also be a graduate of this school. Sure enough the presentation of "the basic" training for being a massage practitioner was unlike the other two schools. Each school had a different intention and therefore a different delivery system for the basic information.

Sitting in this class as a seasoned massage therapist was priceless training for The Massage Business Academy! My intention to design a delivery system for this program, which is a clear answer to graduating massage therapists wanting to start their own business, made the material brand new. I've learned to find what resonates for me in my business. I must always have a beginner's mind and be willing to hear the same information more than once.

RELATIONSHIPS ARE EVERYTHING

The most important note on business relationships is connecting with high achievers and taking your time to build a solid foundation of trust. I've found when I can make connections with high achievers and earn their trust, there is no ceiling on what I can create or accomplish. With the "fake it till you make it" veil that so many people hide behind, sometimes it's a mystery exactly who the true high achievers are… it's like kissing a lot of frogs to get to your prince! When I meet new people I am always genuinely interested in who they are, what they do, why they are doing what they do. I need to hear joy and passion in their story and I need to feel like it's coming from their heart.

At 19, I heard the quote, "In this world there are people who are negatives, equals, and positives. To stay where you're at hang out with equals, but to get to your star, hang out with positives." There have been periods of time where my business seemed to be stagnant and sure enough when I investigated matters I found I had let a negative person creep through the back door! To become successful you must keep a close watch on who you are allowing to participate and contribute. Find the people who magnetize you to a place greater than yourself and release those who don't.

TAKE IMMEDIATE AND CONSISTENT ACTION

A great example of this was my move from Texas to Los Angeles. I discovered my ability to sing at age 9 and I've had the dream of a music career ever since. When I hit my 30's I had this moment where my intuition was screaming at me to move to LA. I came on a four day weekend vacation. I walked into one of LA's finest spas where I was hired on the spot. About an hour later I had put down a deposit and first month's rent on a place to live. Two hours later I'm at LAX airport on the phone telling my mother of this turn of events asking for her input. The words that she said next were like music to my ears. She said, "Yvonne, this all came so easily, it must be from God, so follow His plan." It brings me to tears to know what an incredible support she was to me then and in every critical moment of my life. That's all I needed to be fully committed to my move. This experience taught me a huge lesson that has helped me countless times in my business. To be on an unstoppable course for entrepreneurship you must be tuned into your intuition and take immediate and consistent action. Your spirit literally needs feet to be able to fulfill your vision and make a true difference. Your ACTIONS are those feet!

ONLY SHARE YOUR PLANS WITH YOUR FANS

Being a creative person who has a deep drive to follow my dreams, I am always sharing my ideas with everyone. So, when I went home to Texas, I naturally began sharing my joyful news with my 600 clients, one-by-one. Instantly I learned two things. Sometimes when sharing I get the praise and acknowledgment I am expecting. Sometimes I get a barrage of conflict and negativity.

I received comments from "You are completely insane", to "you are completely courageous to follow this dream", to "So how long are you going to give this a try". The most upsetting interaction was with one of my favorite clients. She was a master financial planner. She made me look at my current standard of living expenses and how I would not have the same life if I moved. Her comment was "the only option you will have is to live in the valley renting a house with a bunch of other people". I didn't know anything about the valley, but I certainly didn't feel supported! I loved this client very much and so her words weighed heavily on my heart. Then I had my ah-ha moment. She loved me too. She wanted to protect me from failure and herself from losing her massage therapist! I concluded my fans believe in me and support me without a personal agenda or attachment.

I immediately used this insight to reinforce my personal commitment and to acknowledge my commitment and gratitude to all my clients. Having been an instructor at my massage school I was able to honor my commitment by personally placing all my clients with new therapists. I still find it challenging to be selective with who I entrust with my plans. I remind myself if someone is building a case for why what I'm doing is insane and will never work because, blah, blah, blah that means that they are NOT a fan. If someone lights up and declares, "You're so courageous!" they ARE a fan.

MY ENTREPRENEURIAL CHALLENGES AND HOW I SOLVE THEM

When one of my biggest challenges, such as time management, follow-up, and consistency cause me to have doubt in myself or my vision I go to my coach! A carefully selected mentor is your fan when you want to throw in the towel. As I mentioned earlier, I've invested in a lot of training. I find that implementing new knowledge and wisdom is 100% easier with a coach. When I go to my trainings I listen on the edge of my chair and I soak up all the information. I ask questions. I take occasional notes. I make sure that everything makes sense to me. Then if I don't have a coach, I go home and a million things come at me. I don't finish the follow-up homework. I don't carve out the time to review my notes. The great skills are now in my tool box, but they are not getting reinforced. Having a coach allows me to be accountable to the goals I set for myself. It calls me to be bigger than my circumstances. I regularly express my challenges with time management and together we find solutions. My coach requires me to track my activities so that I can overcome my follow-up and consistency challenges. She helps me discover new business exercises to build new capacities and reach my goals.

MUST HAVES FOR NAVIGATING ENTREPRENEURSHIP

The most important business advice I have for someone venturing into an unstoppable course of entrepreneurship is to develop CONFIDENCE and CHARISMA. Confidence comes from developing your sensitivity to your intuition and trusting that it is leading you to the next right action. If you need support in building this capacity, share your intuitive hits with your coach who is your biggest fan. Your coach will help you overcome the challenges that are mental, emotional, or spiritual blocks for you. Your coach will give you the practical systems and tools to help you bring your dreams into tangible form. In time your actions will be in line with your intuition and charisma will magically arrive! Allow yourself to live in your business as freely as your personal life. People will see you as you really are... a joyful, vital and passionate UNSTOPPABLE entrepreneur!

LIVE IN GRATITUDE AND EXPRESS ACKNOWLEDGEMENT ALWAYS

A major tip I must also share for navigating entrepreneurship - being grateful and acknowledging others. I personally thrive on a consistent diet of praise cookies! I find that when I shine the light on the contribution people are to me and my business, I get more business. I understand the dynamic behind the result. I feel good when someone is grateful for me and acknowledges my contribution. It makes me feel good. Who doesn't want feel good? So, I am so grateful for all the connections and training that has contributed to my life and the ever expanding resource that is The Massage Business Academy.

Getting back to answering my two questions "why is it that I can always generate clients and create the cash I need when so many other therapists are struggling from the starving healer syndrome?" "Why have I been unstoppable in navigating entrepreneurship and how could I create a path to help?" I see an opportunity to be an *Innovative Woman* by equipping massage therapists to be entrepreneurs instead of employees.

Here's the scenario I've seen too many times…

BURNOUT BEFORE BRILLIANCE

This scenario isn't limited to massage therapists. Many types of practitioners in the healing fields receive insufficient training on the numerous facets of launching, building, and expanding a business. These therapists come out of their training having no internship or space to begin building their own committed clients. Without the experience, the confidence, or capital to invest in opening their office, they revert to becoming an employee. The pay from their job is so minimal that they begin to offer their services to their friends and family on the side at deeply discounted rates. Time passes and they need to work less and earn more. They don't feel good raising their rates for friends and family so they take on more work at their job. Now the stage is set for burn out. There is a lack of recovery time from the physical stress and exertion the work has on their body. Without the recovery time or the funds to nurture their body, energy plummets and so does their attitude. Now the inspiration for healing and serving is greatly diminished. The financial stress seems so great that they become cynical, resigned, and maybe even resentful. They opt to take on odd jobs to pay the bills and when they can't take it anymore, they quit. This is so painful to me. I have received such amazing practitioners who simply didn't get the experiences, training, or opportunities that life has presented to me.

THE SOLUTION

The Massage Business Academy provides massage therapists with the TOOLS, SKILLS, PROCESSES and METHODS to allow their passions to become tangible. TMBA helps them on the practical level, mentoring them to earn the income they deserve for their gifts, talents and skills, BEFORE they ever experience working their fingers to the bone.

Presently, I'm promoting enrollment for The Massage Business Academy. I also have free business analysis and strategy sessions available for massage therapists who feel they have that entrepreneurial calling and are searching for training in earning a healthy five figure income. I am reaching out to my business relationships and expanding my own circle of influence through speaking engagements. If you know a massage therapist who is struggling from the starving healer syndrome please contact me or pass my information on to them. I hold introduction workshops and intensives. Ongoing, new content and expert interviews are being added to the basic training modules available 24-7 for my TMBA students.

ABOUT THE AUTHOR:

Yvonne Larson, Founder of **Absolute Vital Care Bodyworks** in Los Angeles, California, is a Master Massage Therapist with the experience and ability to customize every treatment to the needs of her clients. Best known as "The Neck Work Expert," she has worked in the Health and Beauty industry for more than 20 years. With hundreds of client testimonials to her credit, her mantra is *"Give me ONE visit, I'll earn your business for life!"* Yvonne received her own training at The Institute of Massage & Miracles, Health Masters School of Massage, and The Winter's School. Having studied directly with numerous highly acclaimed and influential masters of energetic bodywork, holistic healing, and the metaphysical disciplines, her style is both unique and special.

Being a consummate entrepreneur, risk-taker, successful business owner and mentor, Yvonne is embarking on an exciting new venture in 2014, **The Massage Business Academy** (TMBA). This comprehensive, six-month program offers proven tools, skills, services, business solutions and training to build confidence and accelerate their success as entrepreneurs. She is currently working on her inaugural book in the TMBA series, and screening applicants for the program commencing this spring.

Yvonne Larson
The Massage Business Academy

(800) 711-4081
www.TheMassageBusinessAcademy.com
yvonne@TheMassageBusinessAcademy.com

STEERING THROUGH THE OBSTACLES TO REACH SUCCESS

By Candy Messer

When I went to college for business management, I didn't have in my mind that I'd ever be an entrepreneur. Although my Grandfather owned a business, I didn't live near him and didn't ever really see what it was like to be a business owner. Everyone else I knew (friends and family) all worked for someone else. However, in late 2002, someone who knew that I was a bookkeeper asked me to help her with the bank reconciliations for her husband's business. She didn't mind posting customer deposits, or paying bills, but in her words, she "hated bank reconciliations."

After months of her requests, I finally relented. I filed for my business license and began helping her. I would pick up the information, do the work at home, and return the backup file to her once the work was complete. I had a happy client and I thought I might as well work with a few more since I had to pay for my license. At that time I was working 3 days a week so I could volunteer in my children's classes at school and get errands done while they were in school. I worked with the few clients I had on the days I didn't have to work my "real job" and when I wasn't at my children's school. After a year and a half of working as an employee and a business owner, my husband suggested I quit my job and focus on my business. I feared leaving the comfort of employment and a guaranteed paycheck, but he continued to encourage me, and I gave my notice.

When I started my business, I had no idea what I should charge. My first client told me what she had paid her previous bookkeeper and that is what I was paid too. My second client was referred by a bookkeeper who had too much work, so I billed the same price she had charged. In 2005 I took over some accounts from a tax preparer who no longer wanted to do the bookkeeping or payroll. When looking at the pricing, I knew my customers were being charged a lot less than other companies charged, but it was difficult to raise prices anywhere near what they should have been as it would have been a significant increase, so I slowly raised prices over the next few years. Even now, some of those clients are still under the level they should be because I don't want to increase rates too much at any one time. I wish I had thought through my pricing when I first started. Although it would have been difficult to raise current clients to a more reasonable level, I could have started new clients at a level more in line with the value of the services I provided. But being new into entrepreneurship, I didn't have the confidence to charge more than what the two bookkeepers for my first two clients had charged (they must not have felt confident enough to ask for higher rates either). My failing to truly analyze what I needed to earn and the value of the services I offered kept me at a lower revenue rate for my company than I should have had. As my business continues to grow and clients see the expertise I have, I am much more confident in asking for a reasonable price for the services I offer.

Another challenge I faced was not setting strict boundaries with clients from the start. Because many of them had been working with someone else and were accustomed to that process, I didn't establish my own guidelines for when and how the work would get to me. This meant that a lot of work came in at the same time and I was overwhelmed. Many would bring it in just before a filing deadline and I'd work long hours to finish everything timely. Because I don't like confrontation, I wouldn't discuss how difficult this made my work schedule. Another boundary I failed to set was payment up front. Because I had no entrepreneurial experience, I just followed the process of the person whose accounts I took over in 2005. She did the work first, invoiced after the project was done, and then the customers would pay (sometimes months later). After having to write off many accounts as bad debt, I realized there had to be a better way to work. So having gone through some issues when starting my business, I want to share some tips with you that will help you become a successful entrepreneur and (hopefully) prevent you from making the same mistakes I made when starting my business.

My first tip is calculate what you need to charge in order to be profitable and have the resources you need in your business. This may need some adjustment, but planning based on key factors will help get close to your target number. If you are a service business, start by calculating how many hours you want to work in a year. A 40 hour work week annually would be 2080 hours. Look at what other days off you might like (vacation, holidays, seminars to attend) and reduce your total available hours by the figure you get from that calculation. The remaining number is the total hours you want to work, but much of that will not be billable time. Reduce your hours by at least 10% (more if you spend a lot of time on tasks that aren't directly billed to clients).

Now determine how much you want to make in a year (be reasonable here. If you are just starting, you may not earn $100,000 in your first year) and take the total revenue you want to earn and divide by your total hours available. This will give you the minimum amount you need to charge in order to hit your goal. Keep in mind that you need to determine if your earnings are gross receipts (before any expenses) or net income that you are calculating. For instance, if you want to generate revenue of $100,000 in the business and you have 2000 hours available, the minimum to bill would be $50.00. However, after you pay all of the business expenses, you may earn significantly less. If you want to generate $100,000 of net income (after all expenses are going to be paid) you'll need to know your estimated expenses for the year, add $100,000 to that total then divide by the available hours to get the billing rage. For instance, if total expenses for the year would be $50,000, then add the desired $100,000 of income to the $50,000 and divide by the available hours to get a billing rate of $75.00 per hour). To set up a budget, go to: http://bit.ly/1aPJmVr

If you are selling products, there are two ways you can determine the minimum price. You can do as explained above (determine total revenue desired and divide by expected number of units to be sold.) This would give the minimum price to charge. However, your expectation of how many will be sold may be overstated. Another method to determine minimum price would be taking total costs per unit, add in the desired profit per until and determine selling price. For instance, if total costs to make one unit are $50 and you want a 50% profit ($25), your minimum sales price would be $75.00. To help with this calculation, see http://bit.ly/1aPJmVr

My second tip is to plan from the start that you'll have someone assisting you in the future and document all of your processes. This will make training them so much easier. You'll have step by step instructions for each assignment that they can easily follow and do the work exactly as you have done. This will make the work output the same no matter who does the process. If you wait until you are ready to hire, the task of writing out all of the systems may be extremely overwhelming. Planning for growth and assistance now will make it so much easier to hire (or outsource to a virtual assistant) in the future.

A third tip is to set your boundaries and stick to them. What are your billing terms? If your type of work requires invoicing after the task is complete, I recommend collecting a deposit up front to cover costs you'll incur (including your time), and when that deposit has been used, request an additional deposit. This will guarantee you will be paid for work you have completed. Have these rules for all clients, even close friends or family members. Often it's those you think won't burn you who end up not paying timely. Establishing rules that all clients follow will make it easier for you and your staff to enforce them (and clients will generally meet your expectations). Also consider if you want to be able to be reached at any time. If not, don't give your cell number (or say that you only take/return calls during set hours). You want customers to respect your free time, and allowing them access to you at any time is not a good idea. You may think it's great customer service, but you may end up resenting that you have no free time if you don't set your business hours from the start.

Bear in mind that most often, the ones calling you at all hours are the ones who don't respect your time. For instance, I had a client who had called on a Thursday afternoon needing three years of bookkeeping done by the following Monday as that was the day the IRS stated an audit was going to be done. This was someone who had stopped using our bookkeeping services three years prior to do the work internally to save money. When the audit notice arrived, they put off doing anything about it until the last minute expecting that it could all be done in a day and a half. Not only did he not consider that I may have had other work already scheduled, he didn't realize that with the amount of transactions he had, it could not be done even if I spent my entire weekend working. I let him know he'd need to ask for an extension as it was impossible to complete within the time frame given. Once the work was complete, he was going to have his CPA review the file and called me on Friday afternoon asking for my cell number so they could call me the next day (which happened to be my husband's birthday). I politely told him that I don't give out my cell number and that I would not be available on the weekend. He was not happy, but it was his failing to get the work done timely in the first place that led to his wanting me to work on the weekends. Had I given in on that boundary, I would not have been happy, my husband would have thought he was less important than my client, and the client would think he could call me at any time.

So think about it...will you want to be called on the weekends, at night, when you are on vacation, or other inconvenient times because you have not set those boundaries with your clients? Most of your clients understand that you operate within business hours and will respect that. Those that don't are probably the ones you won't want to work with anyway. They will most likely be the most demanding and slowest to pay your invoices.

As a woman, I've found that I've run my business more with my heart than my head. Although women are generally more nurturing, I've found that this has had a negative impact on my business. I have tried to be nice to customers, employees, and vendors alike. I feel this is important, and I've developed some great relationships over the years, but my being too kind has caused some customers to think it isn't as important to pay me timely, or employees think they don't actually need to do what I've spelled out as requirements. Instead of nipping the problem in the bud, my kindness prolonged the inevitable. For instance, I had a client who was falling behind in making payments to me but I kept on working on his account. He was going to sell the business and asked if I could be paid from the sale proceeds. Since we had worked together for quite a few years I agreed. Soon after he passed away, the business was shut down rather than sold, and I never received payment. Had I been stricter in my guidelines, I would have either stated that I needed to have the account brought up to date before I did any additional work, or we could have terminated services at that time. Either option would have allowed me to do work and be paid (option 1 would have me paid by my current client, option 2 would allow me to work on another account). Although it is still difficult for me to make decisions with my head rather than my heart, if I want my business to continue to be successful, I need to do the things that will allow me to continue to function profitably. I have employees who are counting on this business to continue. I have an obligation not only to my own family, but to my employees. I'm not saying don't allow emotions to impact your decisions, only that decisions should be reviewed from a logical perspective as well as an emotional one. If you seem to make decisions more from your heart, have an accountability partner you can talk to who you can run through scenarios, make decisions on how it should be handled, and allow you to practice those conversations if necessary. Knowing someone is there to help make these decisions (and make sure you follow through with them) will be quite helpful.

I'm in a place now that I never thought I would be when I started my business. I've begun writing and speaking about topics I feel are important for entrepreneurs. I'm not just doing the work, I'm educating business owners on how to be successful. I have found this to be an exciting new adventure, and I'm looking forward to where this may lead. In order to do this, I need to continue to develop an amazing team in my office so that the work can continue to be done timely. I'm thankful that those I have working for me now are willing to help my business continue to be successful by being trustworthy employees and allowing me to go out and speak to groups and share my expertise. It's because of their hard work that I can do the speaking and writing.

As an innovative woman, I am constantly looking for ways we can offer more value to our clients. That may be finding new applications/technology to make their lives easier, offering new services that will help relieve more of their bookkeeping burden, and educating my clients by sharing important information such as updates to tax laws, so that they can make educated decisions in regards to their businesses.

As an entrepreneur, I encourage you to review your pricing, processes, and boundaries to make sure those are where they should be to ensure your success. Adjust where necessary and understand that those who truly value the products or services you provide will be willing to pay your rates and honor your boundaries. Set yourself up for success now, and live the dream of being a success!

ABOUT THE AUTHOR:

Candy Messer is a bookkeeping and payroll expert who works with entrepreneurs in service-based industries such as fast food services, medical offices, landscaping and interior design. She energizes business owners by removing the burden of the bookkeeping and payroll processing. As a result of using her services, her clients have peace of mind and the freedom to do what they love. With more than 15 years of experience, Candy understands the stresses business owners face and offers customized services to meet their varying needs, including bookkeeping, payroll, QuickBooks ™ consulting and bill pay services.

Candy speaks on topics such as what to know before hiring an employee, the benefits of outsourcing services, and how to become financially savvy. Candy was named Woman of the Year for 2009-2010 by the Peninsula Chapter of the American Business Women's Association. She was named the 2011 Entrepreneur Mom of the Year by Today's Innovative Woman magazine. In 2012, the El Camino College Foundation honored her as a Distinguished Alumni of the Year. She is also a member of the American Institute of Professional Bookkeepers.

Candy Messer
Affordable Bookkeeping and Payroll

Call us today, have peace of mind tonight!
310-534-5577
www.abandp.com
contact@abandp.com

JOURNEY TO SUCCESS

By Stephanie Otero

Hindsight is 20/20. At least for me this rings true. If only I had known 10 years ago what I know now, starting and running my business would have been a heck of a lot easier. But sometimes, it's more about the journey and finding your way. Once you find your way, those experiences you've had, no matter how stressful or painful, become invaluable tools and resources for your future.

Ten years ago, I was working 50-60 hour work weeks and was about to be a mommy for the first time. I didn't know exactly what I wanted for my life, but I knew what I was doing, wasn't it. So, I decided to be a stay at home mom. I envisioned days full of giggles, play dates, gym time, and plenty of dates with Oprah. My dreams were quickly shattered when reality set in. My baby girl was colicky, so giggles were replaced with lots of crying and tears. All of my friends were working and busy moving up with their careers, so I found myself isolated and lonely. I barely had time to take a shower each day, so gym time was certainly out of the question, and sadly, the dates with Oprah were few and far between.

It had been three months since I left the corporate world for mommy-hood, and I had lost myself. I had given up business suits for sweat pants, heels for flip-flops, and showers for quick sponge baths. I no longer recognized myself. I had lost my ability to carry on a conversation with adults. Unless they were interested in the newest *Baby Einstein* DVD or knew anything about how to relieve a baby's gas, well, I frankly had nothing in common with them anymore. I started to doubt my decision to leave the corporate world but then something amazing happened.

My phone rang. It was a client that I had worked with for several years at my corporate job. He was unhappy with the CPA they had assigned to his account and wanted to know would I consider working for him, from home, at my convenience? My answer, "HELL, YES"! I felt like I had just won the freaking lottery! I was going to be able to stay home with my daughter, while working from home? It was genius! I only wondered why I had never thought of it. And so I begin my road to entrepreneurship.

I made all the mistakes a rookie could make and then some. I took every client that came my way. I took every project that came my way. I charged less for my services than my colleagues. I didn't have set business hours. I didn't hire help until I was suffocating with work. The result was one over-worked and one over-tired, *me*.

Eventually, I found my way. I acquired an office, hired an assistant, set office hours, and raised my fees. Ten years later, I had a successful CPA practice in Palm Desert, CA and my practice was growing by leaps and bounds each year. There was just one problem. I had lost all my motivation. Work became a burden. I had no passion for what I was doing. I was tired, burnt out, and just knew that I couldn't do it any longer. So, I closed my practice and walked away from it all.

Closing my business was no easy feat for a Type A, conservative person, like myself. My whole life I played it safe and had a plan. Closing a successful practice and having no plan for the future, is anything but safe. For once in my life, however, I did the unthinkable and took a bold, leap of Faith. I reconnected with myself, my goals, and my aspirations. I spent quality time with family and got back to enjoying the little things. After a few months, I found myself and my passion again.

I knew I wanted to work with business owners, entrepreneurs and non-profit organizations. I have always been good with numbers and accounting is truly a part of my DNA. I know what you're thinking. How can I, or any other sane being, possibly be passionate about numbers? It's not really about the numbers. It's obviously, an inevitable part of what I do, but for me, it's really about communicating and empowering business owners.

Going through the trials and tribulations over the ten years of owning a CPA practice and reconnecting with myself and my passion, has given me so much more focus. It's also led me to a more spiritual, joyful, peaceful, and happier life than I ever imagined possible. And although it was a long, rocky journey to get where I am today, I'm thankful I finally did find my way.

So, when business owners or entrepreneurs ask me if I have any words of wisdom or advice as they start their journey of entrepreneurship, I usually respond with, "How much time have you got?". While I encourage you to fully enjoy your journey and all that you will learn along the way, here are some thoughts to keep in mind and that may provide a short-cut in helping you reach your destination:

BE BOLD AND HAVE FAITH

Every successful entrepreneur or business owner started with one single step – *they were bold and acted on Faith*. They were bold enough to take action, even though they had no clue what the future held for them. I won't lie, it's scary as hell. But, it's also the greatest feeling in the world to know that you are putting Faith in something, better yet, *someone*, that you know has all the capabilities to succeed and cannot fail. That someone is *you*.

"Faith is taking the first step even when you don't see the whole staircase." - Martin Luther King, Jr.

FIND YOUR PASSION AND EMBRACE IT

Before you can embrace your passion, you need to find it. Don't worry if you don't know what it is right now. It may just be that you are trying too hard or you are rejecting the gifts that you have been given because they aren't what your idea of your passion should be. Let me explain. How many times have you heard the phrase, "If you are doing what you love, it won't feel like work?" *(Insert an eye roll here.)* Whenever someone would say that to me, I felt like bonking them over the head! I was doing what I loved, and it always felt like work! So, what did they know or have that I didn't? *They embraced their passion.*

Even though my life had led me to the world of accounting time and time again, I rejected the idea that it was my life's purpose. I thought for sure the big "G-man" had made a mistake with me. I mean, I'm not a boring person. I'm creative, I love to write, and I love people. Those are not accountant-like traits, right? And let's not forget that it's accounting! Could there be anything more un-glamorous? It's math and numbers - two things despised by almost all man-kind! However, it wasn't until I learned to embrace these gifts, that I truly found my passion. Numbers and math play a big part in what I do, but what I didn't realize is they were just the tools necessary that led me to my true passion.

So whether you've already found your passion, are having trouble accepting it, or still need to find it – when you know it, embrace it. For it is once you embrace your passion, that your success will truly start to unfold.

"Always remember, you have within you, the strength, the patience, and the passion to reach for the stars to change the world." – Harriet Tubman

KNOW YOUR VALUE

Whether you are a service based entrepreneur or have a product to offer, you really want to make sure you are valuing your service or product. When I first started my CPA practice, I thought that if I offered my services for a "lower cost" than my colleagues, I would have more business and could grow my practice faster. Yes, I grew my business and I had a lot of clients, but the problem was they were not with me because they "valued" my services. They were with me because I was the "cheapest". You don't want to get clients or customers based on this. It's much more difficult to have your clients see the "value" of what you do later, if they don't see it initially. You've also heard the phrase, "Work smarter not harder?" This is a perfect example. I was working twice as hard as my colleagues for a lot less money.

Also, I'm not saying you need to be the most expensive either, but you do need to know your worth and find a happy medium. Think about what you would pay. This will help you find a price point that you are happy with. And always remember, if a client thinks you are too expensive, that's okay - *they are not the client for you*. You want the clients that know you are worth your fees because they see the "value" in what you have to offer.

> **"Sometimes the hardest part of the journey, is believing you're worthy of the trip." – Glenn Beck**

BE SELECTIVE

Oh boy, this is a big one. When you are just starting out in your business, it's so easy to want to say "yes" to every potential client that comes your way because you think you need to! I made this mistake and the result was having a lot of "baggage" that really weighed me down and used up a lot of my energy.

You can be selective about who you want to work with. There is plenty of business out there for you! When you initially meet with a potential client, it is as much an interview for you as it is for them. The relationship should be mutually beneficial. You should know that you can truly be of service to that client, and that client should see the value in what you have to offer. This is a recipe for a happy, long-lasting, working relationship!

"Learning to say no, can earn you respect from yourself as well as, those around you." – Auliq Ice

NEVER SETTLE

The best part of being "you" is that there is always a better version of you that is growing and learning from your experiences. The best "you" is still yet to come. Don't ever settle or become complacent. When a client tells me or a team member that we are doing a great job, I give myself a pat on the back, but then I think of how I can change that "great" to an "outstanding". I thrive on exceeding others' expectations. If you are always striving to do better and improve, you are not only growing as a person, but you will get the creative juices flowing, which can lead to bigger and better things that you might never had imagined otherwise.

"There is nothing noble in being superior to your fellow man; true nobility is being superior to your former self." – Ernest Hemingway

Remember no matter where you are on your journey, be Bold, have Faith, find your Passion and Embrace It. These are the hard steps, and once you've taken these, you will have a short-cut to your final destination of Success. I wish you endless days of living your passion.

ABOUT THE AUTHOR:

Stephanie Otero is a mom, writer, blogger, business owner, CPA and so much more, depending on the day! After being in the accounting world for 19 years, she decided to follow her heart, live a more meaningful life, and start a new journey in life. This led her to create Wise-Full Heart, which is Stephanie's passion for self-discovery and leading a more meaningful life. Some people may call it a "mid-life crisis"; however, she calls it a "mid-life awakening"! You can follow Stephanie on her journey and read all about her experiences over at www.wisefullheart.com

Stephanie Otero
Founder and Certified Life & Business Coach

www.stephanieotero.com
stephanie@stephanieotero.com

MORE THEM +
LESS YOU = MORE SALES

By Pam Russell

Have you ever walked into a networking event and someone pounces on you and starts hemorrhaging at the mouth about what they sell and how it can benefit you? Or they walk around the room handing out their business card to every single person in the room. Your head is spinning and you often don't know what hit you. Or have you ever had a meeting with a sales rep that comes in and never asks you what YOU need from them but instead runs over at the mouth with what they can do for you? How do they know what you need them to do for you if they haven't even asked YOU?

Sadly this happens all the time. I believe most people do it because they are passionate about their product, services, etc. and want everyone to know about it. That is a good thing but there is a way to make it more impactful when you share the information. I used to pounce and hemorrhage too – then one day I saw the proverbial light. Once I saw that light I stopped the bleeding of information about me, myself and I in meetings and interactions.

Whether your ideal client is a one person business or a large corporation, the fact remains the same. They just don't have time to listen to you ramble on about your long list of services, products, colors, prices, programs, etc. They don't want to hear all about your metal framed windows when they need and want wood framed windows. You didn't know that because you didn't ask them or give them a chance to tell you.

So, what DO they want?

<u>In a Meeting</u>

If I am going to a meeting with a prospect, I do my usual pre-meeting research (see below) and then come up with a few good questions, not all about business, to ask them that pertain to how my services might help them. Try to make it conversational and not interrogational.

- Pre-Meeting Research:
  - o At minimum look at their website. Look at press releases. Look at leadership. Look at products and services they offer.
  - o Research their competitors.
  - o Look at and follow their LinkedIn company page and Twitter account.
  - o Look at the LinkedIn page for the person you are meeting with.

- In the Meeting:
  - o How long have you been with x company? OR How long have you had your own business?
  - o Companies/People have different marketing strategies, how do you decide on yours?
  - o You have a lot of great products/programs on your website. What has worked and hasn't work for you in the past when marketing them?
  - o If I see pictures of kids in their office I will say, "Oh what great looking kids! How old are they? OR If I am meeting them for coffee and I notice a certain college emblem on their keychain I might say, "Oh I see you have a UT keychain. Is that where you went to college?" (Something NON business). This helps you to find a possible personal connection.

o Think of some questions that fit your particular area of expertise and your company's services and products.

I ask a question and then I close my mouth…and LISTEN.

A remarkable thing happens when you listen. You are then able to tailor your 'message' (response) to show them how your services can help them achieve THEIR goals and ease THEIR pain. This allows you to share information about the wood framed windows (that they NEED) instead of the metal framed windows (that they DON'T NEED). They also might reveal something personal about themselves that will allow you to discover a personal connection with them. Some people do business with people solely based on a personal connection they discover with that person. (i.e. same college, kids go to same school, go to same church, both like the color blue, run marathons, scrapbook, etc.)

That's **MORE THEM….LESS YOU**.

> *"Most of the successful people I've known are the ones who do more listening than talking."*
> ~Bernard M. Baruch, **American Economist and Advisor to US Presidents**

At a Networking Event

Most people go to networking events to get business from people there. Fair enough. I would like to encourage you to flip your thinking though. Go there with the mindset of how you can help them get what they need and want. Don't try to sell them – try building a relationship with them. Ask them questions to get to know them. Again, try to keep it conversational and not interrogational.

• How long have you been coming to this group?
• What is your favorite thing about hanging out with this great group?

- Is there anyone here you would like me to introduce you to?
- Do you have any kids?
- What do you do in your spare time?
- I would love to hear what you do in your business.

I ask a question and then I close my mouth…and LISTEN.

Many times I will start a conversation with someone by complimenting them on their outfit, jewelry or hair. Try not to be too ooey gooey gushy about it but give a genuine compliment. I tend to give compliments easily so it comes naturally to me to do this at events too. Find a topic that you feel comfortable with, besides your business, to start up a genuine friendly conversation. Eventually your business will come up and then you can share.

That's **MORE THEM….LESS YOU**.

"I like to define networking as cultivating mutually beneficial, give-and-take, win-win relationships. The end result may be to develop a large and diverse group of people who will gladly and continually refer a lot of business to me, while we do the same for them."
~Bob Burg, Speaker and Author of the Go Giver

In Follow Up

Follow up is so important. Follow up with no pouncing is even more important. Many people in business never follow up with people they connect or meet with. Or they pound these new or existing connections with emails. I have been in sales for over 15 years. I would never use only one method of follow up. I would never send multiple emails in the same week. I unsubscribe from people that pounce via email. As you can see, I am not a fan of using email as your only marketing and/or follow up strategy. Everyone uses email. Email marketing is why direct mail has lost popularity over the past years but is now gaining popularity with increased success rates. I encourage my clients to step out of the inbox. Be different. It's not hard.

- Send a handwritten note. You don't have to write a novel. Short and sweet works just fine. Write it, include a business card, lick it closed, stamp it in the corner, address it and mail it. Try not to sell.
  o After a Networking Event: "Hi Susie, So great to meet you on Tuesday at the X networking event. I look forward to seeing you again soon!"
  o After a Meeting: "Hi Emily, It was great to spend some time with you in our meeting. I enjoyed learning more about your business. I look forward to working with you soon." Easy.
- Make a phone call. Yes, actually pick up the phone and call them. Many times you get voicemail. That's okay. Leave a quick message asking them to get together for coffee or saying it was great to meet them.
- Reach out via social media by following them on Twitter or connecting on LinkedIn. They will know and appreciate the connection.
- Practice at home. Brainstorm to come up with things that work for your product and or services. Think of ways to follow up that make you stand out from the crowd.

Think of creative things that you like and can try in your follow up. It doesn't have to be expensive or elaborate. The main point here is to make sure you follow up in a non-pushy desperate fashion. No pouncing. I truly believe this will get you noticed and that connections will remember you.

That's **MORE THEM....LESS YOU**.

"We must not, in trying to think about how we can make a big difference, ignore the small daily differences we can make which, over time, add up to big differences that we often cannot foresee."
~ **Cecil Beaton, Academy Award Winning Stage and Costume Designer**

I encourage you to take off your pouncing shoes and try a new pair of shoes. The more you practice not pouncing the more comfortable you will be with it and the more success you will achieve. You will start to attract true connections that will establish mutually beneficial relationships in your business and your life. I have met many people since changing my approach that are now wonderful close friends in my business and in my life. You can too.

I refer to the MORE YOU approach as sales repellent. Try the MORE THEM approach and it will attract business and sales not repel it. You will be more successful and much happier. Give it a try.

ABOUT THE AUTHOR:

Pam Russell is an award-winning sales leader and charismatic dynamo with more than 15 years of sales experience. She is passionate about the sales process, goals and inspiring others through her speaking and coaching to achieve sales excellence. She has an infectious personality, positive attitude and is a fan of having fun while learning. Pam loves sharing her expertise, sales processes, etc. with other professionals so they can stop being frustrating and start being successful!

Pam has won numerous sales awards including: Largest Single Order, Highest Average Order Size, Most New Clients in 30 Days, Most New Orders from Existing Clients in 30 Days, the Centurion Award for increasing her sales by $100,000+ in one year and the Silver Award for Outstanding Sales Excellence.

Pam is a native Texan that lives in the Dallas area. She is a single mom, dog lover, entrepreneur, speaker and future author who appreciates a good sense of humor. In addition to being a speaker and a coach, Pam is the owner and President of Proforma Specialty Marketing, a printing and promotional products company that has been in business for nearly a decade.

Pam Russell
Proforma Specialty Marketing

(469) 939-1678
www.Proforma.com
Pam.Russell@proforma.com

THE JOURNEY OF ENTREPRENEURSHIP

By Debbie Saviano

When you look back on your life, it is often done in an attempt to explain - describe – understand the how and why of who you are to-day. Entrepreneurs are a unique breed and are often misinterpreted.

After all, **"Why can't you just be happy with a regular job?"**

If this is familiar, then you are most likely either already an Entrepreneur OR you soon will be. Good for You!

The **Life of an Entrepreneur** is different from those who seek a more traditional career pathway. The Entrepreneur has a passion that burns so deeply that considering a more customary career direction is out of the question.

You are an Entrepreneur if you are
- Driven to pursue a dream.
- Unsatisfied with a conventional career.
- Often misunderstood by those closest to you.
- Motivated to continue the Entrepreneurial journey.

Entrepreneurs must be surrounded with those who "get you" and who are willing to SUPPORT you. This foundation is a critical component to

SUCCESS. It is an ideal reason to be reading this book, as all the authors are not only successful Entrepreneurs, they are here to support and encourage you on the **Journey of ENTREPRENEURSHIP!**

Life's journey is a combination of clear pathways coupled with countless curves in the road, sometimes ones that are bumpy and filled with potholes, while others are smooth and free of debris.
When you are LIVING your life, you are consumed by the moment and for the most part do not stop to internalize the "Lessons" or think about "how this will serve or be of purpose in later years".

However, ALL past experiences DO prepare you for today and as they say, The Good – The Bad and The Ugly! If we are honest with ourselves, the two later usually serve us better than the first.

When I look back on my childhood, I realize, I should never have been successful either personally or professionally.

However, that is the gift of God and the Universe.
We can achieve anything we set out to do.

WE CONTROL OUR DESTINY; THE LIFE OF ENTREPRENEURSHIP!

When I was growing up my daddy worked in the oil fields and that meant we moved constantly. Attending 2-4 schools per year was the norm. Never knowing how long I would be in one place I made friends quickly and it also meant I had to be flexible and adaptable.

Back in "the Day" moving meant putting everything you owned into a mini U-Haul trailer and pulling it behind the car. Your entire bedroom was packed into a couple of boxes.

It meant you had to know "where you were going" as there was no GPS and directions were accomplished via the rumpled state map folded into the glove box.

To this day, I am great with directions and know how to read a map. Unlike some people I can tell you if it is on the NW corner or the SE corner of the Intersection. I won't mention how young I was when I was allowed to drive on those dusty country roads from Texas to California.

These experiences are the foundation of Who We Are!

Travel – Change – Adventure – Meeting People – Learning are all Naturals for me.

What is it that excites you?
What makes you the happiest?

You will find that whatever the answer to that question is it validates you are indeed following your dream. **You ARE an Entrepreneur**!

During my childhood, I navigated space on a PHYSICAL plane and today I am grateful and thanks to technology, I do it VIRTUALLY via Social Media.

Early on, going after dreams and overcoming obstacles was continually modeled for me. With that came my desire to become an Entrepreneur upon retirement from Education after being a Principal of 5 different campuses during my career.

Along my journey of entrepreneurship, I was fortunate to have SO many teachers! Other entrepreneurs who were willing to contribute to my success by sharing their experiences and lessons learned. Making it possible for me to have a much clearer understanding of what was necessary to be a successful entrepreneur.

In this chapter, I want to provide you with some of the same Information - Questions – Thoughts and Actions that have proven beneficial to me in **Navigating Entrepreneurship. Let the Journey Begin……**

Having a clear picture in your mind of where you are going insures a successful arrival. You would not head west, if planning to visit the East Coast. The same is true of doing business. Many Entrepreneurs have a penchant for being easily distracted. In order to avoid being sidetracked and ending up off course, I established a set of criteria to use in deciding if something should be a part of my business.

Prior to making a business decision, these are the questions I ask myself, helping me to maintain focus.
- Does it benefit others?
- Is it possible to do it remotely? (Location Independent)
- Do I have the skills and expertise to serve the need?
- Does it get me excited?
- Will the financial investment help me with the above?

If those questions are a solid yes, then it is more likely it will end up being a flourishing element of the business. If not, I add it to the "IN the Future List" allowing me to revisit it in the future.

ACTION:
Make a list of similar items, which speak to you and your business.
What are 3 – 5 things which will help maintain focus?

Here are some questions that might help as you make the list and also as you steer ahead in Entrepreneurship. If you have already clearly determined what your "Calling Is" then you are On Your Way!
a. What would you do every day if time and money were no object?
b. What do others come to you for?
c. What skills come easily for you?

d. What sections do you gravitate to in a bookstore?

e. When conversing with others what do you like to know about them?

f. When doing _____it makes you happy and feeling satisfied.

g. Something you know for sure about yourself?

h. Do you feel something is missing?

i. Something you want to be known and remembered for?

1. Stay **TRUE to COURSE**

If we know where we are going and we set our sights on the Port of Call, we will arrive! Staying true to course, you must determine where it is you want to go.

➢ What DO you want to DO?

➢ What will make your heart sing?

➢ What does your inner voice / core say you should do?

➢ What are you constantly planning and / or daydreaming about?

ACTIONS:

a. Determine a long range yearly goal

b. Break it down into monthly goals based on what you want to achieve by the end of each quarter

c. Monitor at the end of each month

d. Adjust as needed (see #2)

Research supports that those who write down their goals are 80% more likely to achieve them! Think you would agree, those are great odds.

2. **You need an Updated MAP**

Navigation is one of the critical components of any journey and thus, you must have an updated map to show you the way. Otherwise, you will get detoured or even worse, lost. There are several ways to stay on course and even better; take the most direct route avoiding delays.

ACTIONS:
Get a **YEARLY Wall Calendar**
Using the Goals in #1 write them on the Calendar for easy reminders.

a. Use a highlighter for Speaking – Clients – Product Development-Conferences – Networking – Social Media Management (having a colored coded calendar is an easy Visual)

b. NOTE (Circle) which of these are creating monetization.

c. At the end of each month reflect back on those activities. Which did NOT generate financial gain and then readjust for the upcoming month. This helps determine where time and energy should be spent inside the business.

d. Viewing the previous 30 days, what is 1 thing you realize you should know more about? For the upcoming month identify a way to learn that information.

e. This activity allows for monitoring activities – Actions and RESULTS.

Make a List of **Influencers** in your realm /industry. (2-4)

a. Monitor for opportunities to learn from them. These are the Thought Leaders – the Explorers who have gone before and have strategies and tips for making a similar journey.

b. Set a Google alert with their Names to stay abreast of the content they are producing.

c. Using Social Media Repost – Tweet – Discussions promoting the Content of these Influencers.

d. Monitor their blogs - publications – articles – social media activity take advantage of the learning opportunities. (combine with # 2-d)

3. Ask for DIRECTIONS

As stated before, every route has had others who have taken the Journey before you and most likely have advice and even shortcuts. Heeding direction and pointers from others can save so much time – energy & money! Just as those early explorers discovered faraway places around the globe, there are Entrepreneurial Navigators who can do the same for you.

ACTION:
Develop an **Accountability Partner** or a **Mastermind Group**
   a. Entrepreneurs who are willing to give advice and counsel and who will hold you accountable.
   b. This can be either formal or informal.
   c. Create a regular schedule, which you adhere to.

A popular song "I Wish I Knew Then, What I Know Now" has always resonated as it speaks to what we ALL wish was possible.
However, Life has other plans for us.

Embarking on the **Road to Entrepreneurship** is one that most recognize is inescapable. Thanks to technology, social media and books like this we are able to learn from others who have already navigated the waters.

There is no need to recreate and take on hardships which others have already found solutions for. Thanks to their knowledge and experiences; Entrepreneurship is much easier and more profitable all resulting in a successful business.

Just as in life, there is no perfect journey and there will always be hiccups, however, you also know, there is no other journey you would rather take. Entrepreneurship is one of the most rewarding experiences and here is to wishing you to "**Take the Road less Traveled and May it make All the Difference**!" (Robert Frost)

ABOUT THE AUTHOR:

Debbie Saviano spends her time Helping Professionals "Take Action and Create an On Line Presence by developing • nurturing & maintaining Relationships! With a background In Education and a degree in English, History and Psychology, Debbie implements a practical approach to Social Media. Speaking and Training enable Debbie to remain close to those interested in continuing to learn and embrace Technology as well as innovative methods to build Relationships.

Debbie started out her 1st career driving a yellow school bus and retired after being a Principal of 5 campuses. Today, Debbie Navigates the Virtual Highways and in doing so shows others how to Connect - Engage and Relate to those they can Serve. If you would like to stay in touch and utilize the various Social Media Platforms, please visit www.DebbieSaviano.com/SMLearningLab and please connect on all Social Media Platforms so we might **Continue the Conversations.**

In the words of the Irish Blessing:
"May the Road rise to meet you and the Wind always be at Your Back and until we meet again – May You have Good Luck and Your Pockets be heavy with Coin."
Hugs My Entrepreneurial Friend!

Debbie Saviano
Social Media Learning Lab

(214) 707-2195
www.DebbieSaviano.com
debbie@debbiesaviano.com

NAVIGATING ENTREPRENEURSHIP

By Robin Taney

GET R.E.A.L AND GET NOTICED

Have you ever stopped to think about why you became an entrepreneur? For some, it's in your blood. Your DNA. A family legacy that has been passed down from one generation to the next.

For others, it has been a lifelong dream that started with your first paper route or lemonade stand, and everything you've done since was done with the purpose and intention leading up to this moment.

For many of you, though, the path to entrepreneurship was paved so you could escape from something else. A miserable job, a desperate situation such as a divorce or unexpected financial hardship. The belief that being an entrepreneur has to be better, way better, than whatever you're going through now.

Here's the reality: The road to entrepreneurship is hard. Really hard. It's paved with potholes that will try and swallow you whole. I'm not exaggerating when I say it's not for the faint of heart.

But, sometimes having a heart for something is all it takes to plant the seed.

THE ROAD TO ENTREPRENEURSHIP IS PAVED WITH GOOD INTENTIONS

When I was growing up, I flip-flopped between wanting to be a U.S. senator and a television reporter. I wanted to change the world. (And, in my naiveté, must have thought that being in politics or the media would enable me to do that.)

My resume is like a patchwork quilt—squares in different patterns that when sewn together somehow work. I've been in broadcast news, corporate, nonprofit, event planning, internet marketing, and the tourism and hospitality industries. I've written, promoted, planned, and implemented. I've worked with community leaders, heads of corporations, small businesses and students.

My entire career has revolved around my two passions: writing and relationship building, making public relations a natural fit for me.

Since I was hell bent on changing the world, I focused on entrepreneurs because the research showed they were the fastest growing sector of U.S. based businesses, yet woefully underserved by PR firms.

According to the 2008 Census, nearly half of all U.S. businesses are small businesses with less than 500 employees. (3.6 million have between one and four employees, compared with 90,386 that have between 100 and 499.) Nearly 75 percent are "non employer firms", or self-employed and about half are home-based businesses.

According to Joanne Pratt, author of **Home-based Business: The Hidden Economy**, *"52% of all home-based businesses are in the services industry, a number expected to rise given the number of corporations that are filing bankruptcy, facing severe budget shortages, or undergoing massive layoffs."*

Creative entrepreneurs are defined by John Howkins, author of **The Creative Economy**, as people who *"use creativity to unlock the wealth that lies within themselves"* rather than external capital. Some creative entrepreneurs are defined as "artist in business" meaning both 'an artist who is in business' and 'an entrepreneur whose business is a work of art'.

Whether or not you're a creative entrepreneur by trade, it takes some creativity to navigate your way to success as an entrepreneur. You see, those positive statistics I just mentioned have a dark side and it is this: eight out of 10 entrepreneurs *fail* within the first 18 months.

IT'S ALL ABOUT RELATIONSHIPS

The top three reasons they fail are:
1. *They have no clue who their customer is.*
2. Their product or service doesn't stand out in the marketplace (no unique value proposition)
3. They fail to communicate these value propositions in a way that compels people to buy.

PR is not about making the front page of the paper or the lead story on the news. It is not fluff. It is not the Teflon coating on a breaking story.

It's about *building relationships* with people who want or need what you are selling. It's about identifying more people like them who will tell their friends. It's about connecting and engaging with these people on multiple levels, so the circle continues to grow, yet still makes everyone feel like they are the ONLY one.

Unfortunately, PR is a mystery to many entrepreneurs. They either view it as something they'll get to when they get to it or dismiss it entirely because they already have enough to do.

IF YOU BUILD IT, WILL THEY COME?

You've worked hard to nurture your dream to reality. You've poured your heart into it (and, I'm willing to bet, a lot of blood, sweat, and tears.) You have this great business that you love, but do you ever feel like your ideal client has no clue who you are? Do you feel like you're always busy, but not really serving the people you started the business for?

What if I told you that your ideal client is out there, and that in order to find him/her, you do NOT need to run naked through the streets, leap from tall buildings, or engage in any type of behavior that would cause your children to claim they don't know you?

What if I told you that you just need to **Get R.E.A.L.**$_{TM}$?

That's right. If you want to work with clients who appreciate you and inspire you to do your best work instead of sucking the life out of you, you need to **Get R.E.A.L.**$_{TM}$
- You need to be **realistic.**
- You need to be **engaging.**
- You need to be **authentic.**
- And, you need to be of the mindset that you want to have a **long-lasting** relationship with your clients.

These four core principles are the foundation of every great business, and I promise you that if you implement them in yours, you will get all the clients you could ever want.

BE REALISTIC

This might be hard for you, especially if you grew up hearing people tell you to "stop dreaming and be realistic."

When I married my (maddeningly) practical husband, he'd been listening to me for years go on and on about how I wanted to start my own business.

And, he'd recite the "practical" statistics that say historically, small businesses don't survive.

Ha! What does he know? When I finally started my business, I had visions that I would be a cross between the Wonder Women of Productivity and MacGyver, accomplishing far more between the hours of 9:00 a.m. and 3:00 p.m. than I ever had in my previous 40-hour life and, with two candy bars, a piece of string and a rubber band, I'd also able to whip up a Halloween costume, get dinner on the table, and clean the house.

So, suffice it to say, it was a little disheartening to have my husband come home from work, see the house a wreck and the laundry not done and ask "What did you do all day?"

As entrepreneurs, we want what we want and we want it NOW, but for the interest of your (and your family's) sanity, please ask yourself these questions:

1. **What are your expectations and when do you want to achieve them by?** Do you want to be on *Good Morning America*, the front page of the *New York Times*, the keynote speaker at a major convention? Are you hoping to be seen by thousands or millions of potential new customers? Or would you just be happy to add 100 new names to your mailing list each month?

2. **What are your obstacles and challenges?** Let's be honest. We all have them. Some are out of our control like financial or family issues, but other obstacles…are caused by us. I remember when I was in Washington D.C. as part of Northwestern University's journalism program, and the news director at a podunk television station told me I would *never* make it as a television reporter. For years, I heard his voice taunting me, even after I went into producing and won the **"Best Newscast"** award by the *Alabama Associated Press* and produced 10 hours of live coverage following a devastating tornado.

It's called self-sabotage, and whether it's the result of former bosses or fears drilled into you since childhood, it's time to face those demons and say "Enough!" Harness that fear and make it work for you. Get comfortable with being uncomfortable because the day you are not scared is the day you stop growing. So, embrace it!

3. **What are you willing to commit to in terms of time and/or money to achieve your expectations?** Do you need to learn social media, but don't have the time? Do you need to hire someone, but don't want to invest the money? If you're not willing *to do whatever it takes,* you won't achieve your expectations.

TIP: At the end of each year, start planning for the next. What worked and what didn't? What events are you attending or speaking at where you can leverage the power of PR? Having a plan in place makes it a lot easier to spot opportunities where you can find and be found by your ideal client.

BE ENGAGING

Instead of marketing to the masses and getting lost in the noise, reach out to your ideal customer at the precise moment they need what you're offering.

Have you ever been searching for something in a store, and thought you were going to lose your mind because nothing was quite right? And, then, just when you're about to give up, the perfect item appears, seemingly out of nowhere.

When you engage with your ideal customer, you don't just appear. You've been there all along, listening and asking questions. Your ideal customer trusts you because you're not like the others who are just out to make a sale. Jill Bates of Crystal Clear Consulting puts price, quality, and service at the forefront of every interaction she has with clients, from her early days working with brides to make their dream dress to consulting with businesses on how to market themselves.

"I tell people right up front what my services will cost," she says. "When you're confident, you can charge more."

TIP: Create a profile for your ideal customer. Be really, really specific. Give them an identity. What kind of car do they drive? Where did they go to school? What do they do for work? Fun?

Figure out what problem/need they have (and they all have one)…and how your product/service can solve it. Then, give them custom content that prompts them to take action.

10 WAYS TO MAXIMIZE CUSTOMER ENGAGEMENT

Consider this: On average, it takes seven to nine points of contact before a prospect becomes a customer. It's like a courtship. Think about how many times you interacted with your spouse or partner before you/they said "yes."

Customer engagement works the same way. By maximizing every interaction with your prospects and customers and making them serve more than one purpose, you'll find and be found by more of your ideal clients faster. Here are 10 tips to help you maximize every move:

1. Define the **WHO** and that will determine the **WHAT** and **WHERE**
2. Make sure your communication is concept and keyword-focused on your ideal client
3. Use social media outlets that your **ideal clients** and **influencers** are using
4. Spend time getting to know the people you're engaging with
5. Actively participate in **strategic partner groups** (like on LinkedIn)

6. Take a methodical and intentional approach when communicating with your top five key audiences
7. Don't get stuck in the cycle of planning
8. Think about what's right for your prospect, not just what's right for a sale
9. Evaluate why one post is **more engaging** than another
10. Measure before you move forward and then adapt as the needs of your ideal client change

The ultimate goal in this is a sort of customer evangelism, if you will. Get your ideal client to talk about you more than you do because he/she has friends who rely on "word of mouth" *recommendations.

*According to the BIA/Kelsey Consumer Commerce Monitor™ Commerce study released in September, 2013, 94 percent of the consumers surveyed researched a local shopping purchase online; 59.5 percent completed a local purchase of merchandise or services online, and 65.9 percent preferred to make the purchase in-person.

BE AUTHENTIC

All. The. Time.

Being authentic means being transparent and having integrity. If your customers feel they can't trust you, they'll go somewhere else. So, if you mess up, fix it. Remember, social media is like a lit match in a pile of newspaper. It doesn't take long for bad customer service to spread like wildfire. Consumers are willing to forgive a mistake. What they are less willing to forgive is one that's badly handled, or worse, covered up.

FIVE WAYS TO BE AUTHENTIC

1. **Be a resource for information** —Post interesting articles on your blog, offer to write guest posts on other blogs, put together a newsletter. Do whatever you have to in order to keep your ideal clients coming back for more content.

2. **Stop selling and start serving** — Listen to what your ideal prospects are saying on social media and in networking groups. When they mention a problem, you can offer a solution. Post a question and use their answers as content for an upcoming blog post. Share it with the ones you featured and they will in turn share it with their networks.

3. **Be grateful** — How do you thank your customers, contacts, suppliers, etc.? Let them know how much you appreciate them by delivering superior customer service, listening to their needs, and being responsive. I shared a blog post, 22 Reasons I'm Thankful, with my social networks and got a lot of traffic just because the people I featured shared it with their networks. Everyone loves to feel loved.

4. **Be vulnerable** —In other words, be so sure of what your business stands for that you will not compromise. Dr. Brené Brown, author of _Daring Greatly: How the Courage to Be Vulnerable Transforms the Way We Live, Love, Parent, and Lead_ says vulnerability is about being all in. "It's a willingness to show up, be seen and take chances," she says.

5. **Start with who you know** —Leverage your relationships with friends, family, and current business associates. Word of mouth is one of the most effective forms of PR. Add in the power of social media and you have "word of mouth" on steroids.

BEING AUTHENTIC MEANS BEING WILLING TO STAND BEHIND YOUR PRINCIPLES EVEN IF IT MEANS LOSING CUSTOMERS.

Take General Mills, the makers of Cheerios, which aired a commercial on YouTube featuring a mixed race family. The company received a lot of racist comments by people who were offended. Cheerios, however, was unfazed and continued to run the commercial, saying they recognize there are many types of families and celebrate them all.

HOWEVER, BEING AUTHENTIC CAN ALSO BACKFIRE.

Such is the case with Abercrombie and Fitch, the clothing retailer known for its classic and preppy style. A magazine interview that CEO Mike Jeffries did in 2005 resurfaced on social media. In it, he said the reason the retailer doesn't sell clothes in plus sizes is because he doesn't want plus-sized people shopping in his stores. He only wants "beautiful people" wearing his clothes. This caused such a huge backlash on social media that many people boycotted the brand and gave their clothes to the homeless.

DEVELOP A LONG LASTING MINDSET

Close your eyes. Imagine that you're seated in a room with a lot of people you know, but they can't see you. Each person goes to the front of the room to say a few words. What are they talking about? They are giving the eulogy at the funeral of your business. What would your customers say? Would they say they are devastated your business is gone? What about your employees? Would they say they felt appreciated and empowered to do their best work? How about your family? Would they say that even though you worked really hard to provide for them, you still had time for them?

To have a long lasting relationship with your ideal customer, you need to be in sync. It's like rowing a boat. A crew team has to put its oars in the water at the same time every time. If anyone is off, everyone is off.

THREE WAYS TO BUILD A LONG-LASTING RELATIONSHIP WITH YOUR IDEAL CUSTOMER

1. **Be a Thought Leader** -- It's not enough to promote yourself as an "expert". You have to back it up. When you have a dynamic website, blog or podcast series packed with great content and innovative ideas, it brands you as a thought leader who is smart, understands the market and would be a valuable person to do business with.

2. **Have a Servant Attitude** -- When you come from a place of service rather than selling, people will see that you have integrity and will trust you.

3. **Give with No Strings Attached** -- Give away information for free that you'd feel comfortable charging a few hundred dollars for. You will gain credibility and loyalty with your buyers who will happily tell their friends who will tell their friends, etc.

Navigating entrepreneurship is not easy. Throughout this journey, you may find yourself questioning your choice many times.

But, you have *something* special to offer that no one else can. Focus on that and hire people to help you with the stuff you don't know.

I guarantee that if you **Get R.E.A.L**, you *will* get noticed and you will be found by your ideal client. I'll be watching.

ABOUT THE AUTHOR:

Robin Taney, owner and founder of Studio 4 PR, teaches women entrepreneurs that in order to find and be found by their ideal client, they need to **Get R.E.A.L.**$_{TM}$. They need to be realistic, engaging, authentic, and of the mindset that they want to have a long-lasting relationship with their clients. (In other words, they need to be real.) She offers one on one consulting, group programs, an online PR bootcamp, workshops and is available to speak.

Sign up for her mailing list at www.studio4pr.wordpress.com and receive three gifts to help your business get noticed.

Robin Taney
aka The "Get R.E.A.L" Girl
Studio 4 PR

585-705-0500
www.studio4pr.wordpress.com
www.facebook.com/TheGetREALGirl
www.twitter.com/studio4pr
www.linkedin.com/in/robintaney
www.pinterest.com/studio4pr
www.studio4pr.com
robin@studio4pr.com

QUIT? THAT NEVER OCCURRED TO ME!

By Michele Pariza Wacek

I believe there are 2 types of entrepreneurs.

The first type is what I call "traditional entrepreneurs" -- these are folks who love business for business sake. They tend to start businesses because they see an opportunity or a need, not because they have a passion for what the business does. They just love business (which is why many of them tend to be serial entrepreneurs).

The second type goes by many names -- accidental entrepreneurs, conscious entrepreneurs, creative entrepreneurs, messengers, message-driven entrepreneurs, agents of change and more. These entrepreneurs aren't passionate about the business side of the business – they're passionate about what the business does. Maybe they have a big message they want to get out into the world and the fastest way they see that happening is through owning a business. Maybe they want to help people (and the world) transform through their gifts. Or maybe they're passionate about something they do -- such as being a massage therapist or a graphic designer -- and want to build a business around that.

The challenge for the second type is while they may be very good at whatever the business does, they're NOT very good at business. (Either because they don't know or they don't care or it's not their genius and they just want to live in their genius.) Because they're not good at business, they tend to struggle a lot more than someone who is a "traditional entrepreneur."

If this is you (and if you're a woman entrepreneur reading this, I would bet this feels pretty familiar as I've found more women fall into the conscious entrepreneur category than not) then know you're not alone. Lots and lots of now-successful female entrepreneurs have not only found themselves here but have also found their way out. And also know this is an easier fix than you think. Even if you're struggling right now, even if thinking about "biz things" gives you a headache -- you CAN learn enough of the basics to turn your business into one that's successful and profitable.

How do I know this? Because I was once in this category too.

My story starts when I was 3 years old and taught myself to read because I wanted to write fiction so badly. I spent high school and college casting around trying to figure out how else I could make a living writing while I worked on my novels.

Everyone told me to become a journalist. That was the last thing I wanted to be so I kept searching. And then, in college, I stumbled onto this entire world of copywriting.

So what is copywriting? Copywriting is writing promotional materials for businesses. It has nothing to do with protecting intellectual property or putting a copyright on something like a song or a piece of art (note the difference in spelling).

Now, before I go any further, let me say a few words about this entire copywriting industry. You see, businesses need a lot of things written. But most of it is not regular work, which is why a lot of writing is outsourced to freelancers rather than hiring a bunch of writers as employees. Hence the freelance copywriting industry was born.

I stumbled upon this industry pretty much by accident while still in college. Actually, it would be more appropriate to say freelance copywriting found me -- freelance jobs started flowing to me while I was still in college.

"This is great," I thought, "I should make a career out of this."

Which is exactly what I did. At first I balanced being an employee with my freelance projects (and worked on freelance gigs between jobs) until finally in 1998 I started my freelance copywriting business in earnest.

No stop gap. No fooling around. This was it – this was how I was going to make money.

I was the classic entrepreneur who started a business around my gifts -- and I remember even thinking back then I didn't really care for business. But I didn't know what else to do to really pursue my writing career.

So you can imagine my confusion when a few years into my freelance writing business, in 2003, I got that restless feeling. You know that feeling -- it's the one that tells you what you're doing isn't quite right and it's time to make a change/uplevel/stop hiding/etc.

At first I misdiagnosed what was going on. I thought it was because I wanted bigger jobs and to be making more money. At the time I had mostly local clients. Perhaps I needed to go find bigger clients. And that led me to the Internet.

Now here's where it gets interesting. At the same time I started learning and educating myself on how to market myself on the Internet, my local clients started going away. And no new local clients came on to replace them.

At first I was happy. That MUST mean I was on the right path, right? And by having my local clients leave, that MUST mean I was about to get all these new bigger clients.

Right?

Well…

What followed was one of the worst periods in my business. For 6 months my business just died. I was barely making a thousand dollars a month. I remember I had one client who owed me about $300 and it took months to get them to pay me. I was so stressed that I couldn't get that $300 it almost made me sick.

I became quite depressed. I had a lot trouble focusing or getting anything done. It would take me hours to complete simple tasks. I wasn't building any momentum, I was just sinking lower and lower.

It got so bad my husband finally looked at me one day and said "This doesn't seem to be working anymore. Are you sure you want to be doing this? Or do you think you should get a job?"

That stopped me. Quit? It never occurred to me to quit. Even though I was seriously depressed and stressed about how nothing seemed to be working quitting had never been a part of the equation. I thought about that all night. What did I want to do?

And that's when I realized what I wanted to do. I wanted my own business. But somehow in this switch from local clients to marketing online I had lost my way. I wasn't doing everything I knew I should be doing. (Actually I had just about stopped doing everything that I knew I should be doing.) I had allowed my depression over the lack of work to color my entire life.

So I recommitted myself to my business. And less than a month later everything turned around. I landed a few big clients and ended up making up all my lost income in the second half of 2004.

However, the restless still didn't go away. What on earth was the problem? I was a freelance copywriter -- I had the exact same business as other freelance copywriters. What was the problem? Why should I be restless?

It took another year for the answer to finally hit me. I was an entrepreneur. Not just a freelance writer. Yes I am a writer and yes I need to be writing to be happy (and yes I've written 2 novels) but my path is much bigger than what I can accomplish as a writer. I needed to transform myself into an entrepreneur and build a direct response copywriting and marketing business. Only by doing that could I begin to reach the number of people and help the number of business owners and entrepreneurs I'm meant to help.

After I realized this, my first thought was excitement -- YES! This is what I'm meant to do -- build a direct response copywriting and marketing company.

My second thought was "oh crap" -- I have no idea how to go about doing that. I only knew what a freelance copywriting business looked like -- that's what all my friends had, that's what I had. So how do I transform a one-woman copy shop to an actual company?

Well, I can tell you it wasn't without a lot of trial and error since I was very much breaking new ground, but here are the top 3 things I did and what I wish I knew sooner:

1. Business is not a four-letter word. It's actually eight letters. Seriously, though, it really doesn't have to be difficult or scary or boring to actually learn about business. You see, for so long I had resisted learning about business because I was convinced I had no interest in it. However, when I started down the path of transforming my biz into a copywriting and marketing company, I realized two things -- that I had no choice, if I wanted to make this switch I had to learn about biz, but also it wasn't as difficult or as scary or as boring

as I had assumed it would be. It was actually pretty interesting. AND I actually knew more than I gave myself credit for. The more I thought of myself as a business owner rather than a writer who happened to have a business, the more I was able to actually stand in my power and build an actual profitable business.

2. Get creative. If you're a solopreneur like me – doing the work your business does -- you may not have a clue what it would look like if you acted as a business owner rather than one of the employees. (Which is what you are if you're the one doing all the work.) I know I didn't – none of my freelance writer friends had anything that looked remotely what I was trying to build. So I had to look in other industries to model. If you're intrigued by this, I would encourage you to look at other industries as well to see what you can learn or apply to your business. I would also encourage you to get creative -- maybe even play the "what if" game -- what if you had a business where you did NONE of the work? What would that look like? Even if you have no desire to have a business like that, play around with that exercise anyway. What you discover may surprise you.

3. Be prepared to question everything. And I mean everything. INCLUDING your own beliefs (for instance, maybe you're saying to yourself "but Michele, people want to work with me, not with some-one else." Are you absolutely SURE that needs to be true?) Probably the biggest thing I had to personally struggle with were blocks so intertwined in my story I couldn't even see they were blocks. People would question me and I still couldn't see it. What ended up hap-pening with me is the Universe stepped in and whacked me on the side of the head with a 2x4 a few times and that got me to come around. However, if you'd like to avoid the 2x4 I would encourage you to be more open to questions and challenges from your other entrepreneurial friends and coaches.

But the biggest thing I'd like to leave you with is this: If you're feeling called to be bigger than who you are, if you know you're meant to help more people than you are right now, even if you have no idea how this is all going to work, then play around with what I shared here and in my special report. You may be surprised at what comes up for you.

Remember that saying "leap and the net will appear?" Sometimes all you need to do is take one tiny step -- and maybe it's as simple as just letting the Universe know you're open to stepping into your destiny -- and your whole world starts to change.

And when that happens, you'll know you're finally on the right path.

ABOUT THE AUTHOR:

Considered one of the hottest marketing strategists today, Michele PW has a reputation for crafting promotional materials and creating marketing campaigns that get results. She is the owner and founder of Michele PW/ Creative Concepts and Copywriting LLC, which is the premiere international direct response copywriting and marketing company around.

She's also a national speaker and author, plus her client list reads like the "Who's Who" list of Internet marketing.

Michele Pariza Wacek
Michele PW

(877)754-3384
www.MichelePW.com
info@MichelePW.com

This book is a publication of Alessandra Media Group LLC, publishers of Today's Innovative Woman magazine.

Today's Innovative Woman is a print and online magazine serving women entrepreneurs with the latest tips and hottest trends in business! To claim your FREE print or online subscription to the magazine, go to www.TodaysInnovativeWoman.com.

Made in the USA
San Bernardino, CA
22 July 2014